Women in Power at the UN

Women in Power at the UN

Stories to Inspire

Avril David and Shana Sung

ISBN 13: 978-1460934005
ISBN 10: 1460934008

Printed in the United States of America

Dedicated to you, the reader.

Table of Contents

Acknowledgments

There are many people to whom we owe our deepest gratitude for making this book possible.

First and foremost, we would like to thank the honorable women we profiled in this book. Radhika Coomaraswamy, Angela Kane, Susana Malcorra, Rachel Mayanja, and Patricia O'Brien have been most gracious in sharing their time, life stories, and wisdom with the authors and with the many people worldwide who will be reading their stories. Without their contributions, this book would simply not have been possible.

Second, we would like to thank the following staff of the United Nations: Maria Arkoncel, Angeli Badelles, Remeshan Chandroth, Michelle Claudio, Benedicte De Treverret, Roxana Garcia, Chulho Hyun, Tun Khine, Nicola Koch, Timothy La Rose, Itai Madamombe, Masumi Ono, Jose Restrepo, Phyllis Roberts, Pio Smith, and Frank Smyth. We appreciate their kindness and patience in scheduling our interviews, getting us in touch with appropriate contact persons, and working with us to coordinate the publication process.

We received additional help in the production of this book from external interviewers, designers, and editors, including Joanne Asala, Seyoung Baek, Jungwon Choi, Jennifer Hegarty, and Malgorzata Steiner. We appreciate their talents, support, and dedication towards the completion of this book.

Finally, we would like to express our sincere appreciation to Secretary-General Ban Ki-moon, whose commitment to hiring capable women leaders has motivated the authors to introduce to the world some of the remarkable women working for the organization. His genuine commitment and leadership on gender issues have been a true inspiration.

Introduction

Being an Empowered Woman

What do we mean when we say "women in power"? The word "power" is a difficult one to define. According to the *Oxford English Dictionary* (2011), the word "power" has multiple meanings, among them "the ability or opportunity to do something," "the right or authority of an individual or group to do something," and "the ability to control people or things."

Throughout the ages, many great thinkers have offered their perspectives on that last meaning of power — the ability to control people or things. While power can be exercised to influence people for better, it can also be used to coerce them for worse. British historian and moralist Sir John Dalberg-Acton (1834–1902) famously observed, "Power tends to corrupt; absolute power corrupts absolutely."

When we say "women in power," we are choosing to emphasize the more positive aspects of power — namely, the ability "to do" or to act, whether the action is made independently or in cooperation with others; whether in compliance with or in defiance of traditional customs and laws.

We began the quest to write this book with the general assumption that the women in senior positions at the United Nations possess power "to do" many things to improve the state of the world, from fighting poverty to improving the lives of other women. Against the backdrop of historical gender inequalities and widespread disempowerment throughout the globe, we wanted to see how select women were able to attain positions of power in one of the most complex organizations in the world, and how, once in office, they use that power to make an impact.

At the time we embarked on this idea, there were some dozen women in the Senior Management Group of the UN,[i] thanks mostly to Secretary-General Ban Ki-moon, who has set the record by increasing the number of women in senior posts by 40 percent during the last three years. Among the many capable managers, we selected Radhika Coomaraswamy, Angela Kane, Susana Malcorra, Rachel Mayanja, and Patricia O'Brien to profile in this book because of the ethnic and regional diversity that they represent, their geographic proximity to the authors in New York, and their gracious willingness to meet with us.

In the interviews leading up to the development of their unique stories, we sought to delve into who these women are (both culturally and personally), as well as how they had developed professionally over time. We also sought to understand how they viewed and exercised leadership in the context of their positions of power and their status as women.

In writing their stories, we hoped to provide a holistic picture of these women, not only as women with institutional power, but also as wives, mothers, daughters, sisters, and friends. What we gained exceeded our expectations. By speaking with these women in depth, we developed and expanded our understanding of what it means to be "women in power." The term "women in power" does not only refer to those who have the recognized ability to achieve certain status or the authority to influence others. Powerful women are those who are able and willing to lead their lives in an *empowered way,* by making conscious choices to overcome difficulties and make the most out of given circumstances.

In essence, we learned how the socially esteemed titles that

i. The SMG is a committee of senior managers that serves as the secretary-general's cabinet and the central policy planning body of the UN. Its objective is to ensure strategic coherence and direction in the work of the organization. Source: *http://www.un.org/sg/management.shtml.*

these women are bestowed with are external manifestations of what they have cultivated within. As the Roman philosopher Seneca the Younger (c. 1BC–65AD) said, "Most powerful is he who has himself in his own power."

In each profile, we emphasized one theme that we felt captured the core of what each one of these women taught us about what it means to be an empowered woman: Staying True to Yourself, Being a Woman, Finding Your Path, Finding Balance, and Staying Positive.

The first theme, Staying True to Yourself, means being able to answer the questions "who am I?" and "what do I believe in?" An empowered woman knows and is true to who she is and what she believes in, despite external pressures to be or believe otherwise. Being able to answer this question honestly is what enables one to identify and carry out one's true purpose.

The second theme, Being a Woman, emphasizes carrying out one's purpose without denying one's gender. An empowered woman is one who freely and wholeheartedly performs the various roles that her life requires as a professional and a woman, without hindrance caused by the fear or reality of gender stereotypes and discrimination.

The third theme, Finding Your Path, means exercising the freedom to decide what one will do in life based on one's own unique set of interests, goals, and aspirations. An empowered woman is free to discover and choose her own path, to study what she wants to, to pursue the work that she wants to, and to change course, if so desired.

The fourth theme, Finding Balance, means being able to answer the question "what will I dedicate myself to?" An empowered woman is free to focus on all of the things in life that matter to her most. It is the freedom to choose what commitments, both personal and professional, to bring into one's own life and to give each one of those commitments as much passion and dedication as one chooses.

Finally, the fifth theme, Staying Positive, means believing that one has agency to create the life that one wants. An empowered woman is optimistic about her own future, because she knows that her future is in no way limited by her past. This requires an internal resilience that she must cultivate on her own, as well as the legal rights and external support structures that facilitate her ability to make her dreams a reality.

We hope that you, the reader, will benefit from knowing the stories of these exceptional women as much as we did.

Avril David and Shana Sung
March 2011

The United Nations

The United Nations

Historical Background

The idea of establishing the United Nations was conceived during World War II, when the Allied nations found it essential to cooperate in their fight against the Axis powers. In 1941, US President Franklin Roosevelt and British Prime Minister Winston Churchill took the initiative and proposed a set of principles for renewed international collaboration in the Atlantic Charter. In the following year, 26 Allied nations pledged their support for the charter by signing the Declaration by United Nations, the term coined by Roosevelt. This was further supported by the Moscow Declaration on General Security in 1943, in which the Big Four—China, Great Britain, the Soviet Union, and the US—recognized "the necessity of establishing at the earliest practicable date a general international organization"[1] to succeed the short-lived League of Nations.

The Big Four reconvened at Dumbarton Oaks in Washington, DC, in the fall of 1944 and agreed on the Dumbarton Oaks Proposals, containing the aims, structure, and functioning of a world organization. At the Yalta Conference in the Russian Crimean in February 1945, Roosevelt, Churchill, and Joseph Stalin resolved the lingering differences over the organization's operation, giving veto power over "non-procedural matters" to the permanent members of the Security Council, namely China, Great Britain, France, Russia, and the US.

In April 1945, delegates of 50 nations met in San Francisco for the UN Conference on International Organization and drafted the UN Charter. The charter was signed on June 26, 1945 by 51 nations, and the UN came into being on October 24, 1945, with the ratification of the charter by all permanent members and the majority (29) of other signatories.

UN Charter

Born out of the scourge of two world wars, the UN Charter clearly states that the organization's cardinal purpose is "to maintain international peace and security." Other purposes enumerated in the charter are "to develop friendly relations among nations," "to achieve international cooperation in solving international problems of an economic, social, cultural, or humanitarian nature," and "to be a center for harmonizing the actions of nations" (Article 1). The charter also prescribes the convention for dealing with threats to and breaches of peace and acts of aggression.

More importantly, it enshrines a set of principles that define a new era for international cooperation. These principles are sovereign equality of all UN members, good-faith implementation of the charter obligations, peaceful settlement of international disputes, no threat or use of force for aggressive purposes, support for UN enforcement action, and respect for domestic jurisdiction (Article 2).

Principal Organs

To realize the ideals and purposes of the UN, the charter mandates the establishment of six principal organs: a General Assembly, a Security Council, an Economic and Social Council (ECOSOC), a Trusteeship Council, an International Court of Justice, and a Secretariat (Article 7).

The General Assembly, which consists of all members of the UN with equal voting rights, discusses and makes recommendations to the UN member states on any matters within the scope of the charter, except those on which the Security Council is already exercising its functions. Dubbed a "Global Parliament" and "Town Meeting of the World," the General Assembly "effuses the democratic ethos of egalitarianism, parliamentary, or representative government, and majority decision making."[2]

The Security Council, on the other hand, is comprised of five permanent members—China, France, Great Britain, Russia, and the US—and 10 non-permanent members that are elected each year by the General Assembly for a term of two years. The Security Council has "primary responsibility for the maintenance of international peace and security" (Article 24), with the Permanent 5 (P5) exercising veto power over "non-procedural" matters.

Consisting of 54 members from different regions, ECOSOC is charged with advancing economic, social, and human rights progress throughout the world. It produces studies and reports on pertinent issues, convenes international conferences, and makes recommendations to the General Assembly.

The Trusteeship Council was set up to supervise the governance of trust territories by administrating states. With the independence of the last trust territory, Palau, in 1994, the council has completed its entrusted task; it will be officially abolished after the approval of a charter amendment.

The International Court of Justice is the judicial organ of the UN, whose fifteen judges in The Hague decide on cases submitted to it by member states and give advisory opinions on legal questions to the General Assembly, the Security Council, and other UN organs and specialized agencies.

Finally, headed by the secretary-general, the UN Secretariat consists of some 44,000 international civil servants who perform not only administrative and housekeeping duties, but also field missions, including peacekeeping, humanitarian relief, and capacity-building. The secretariat staff are recruited individually

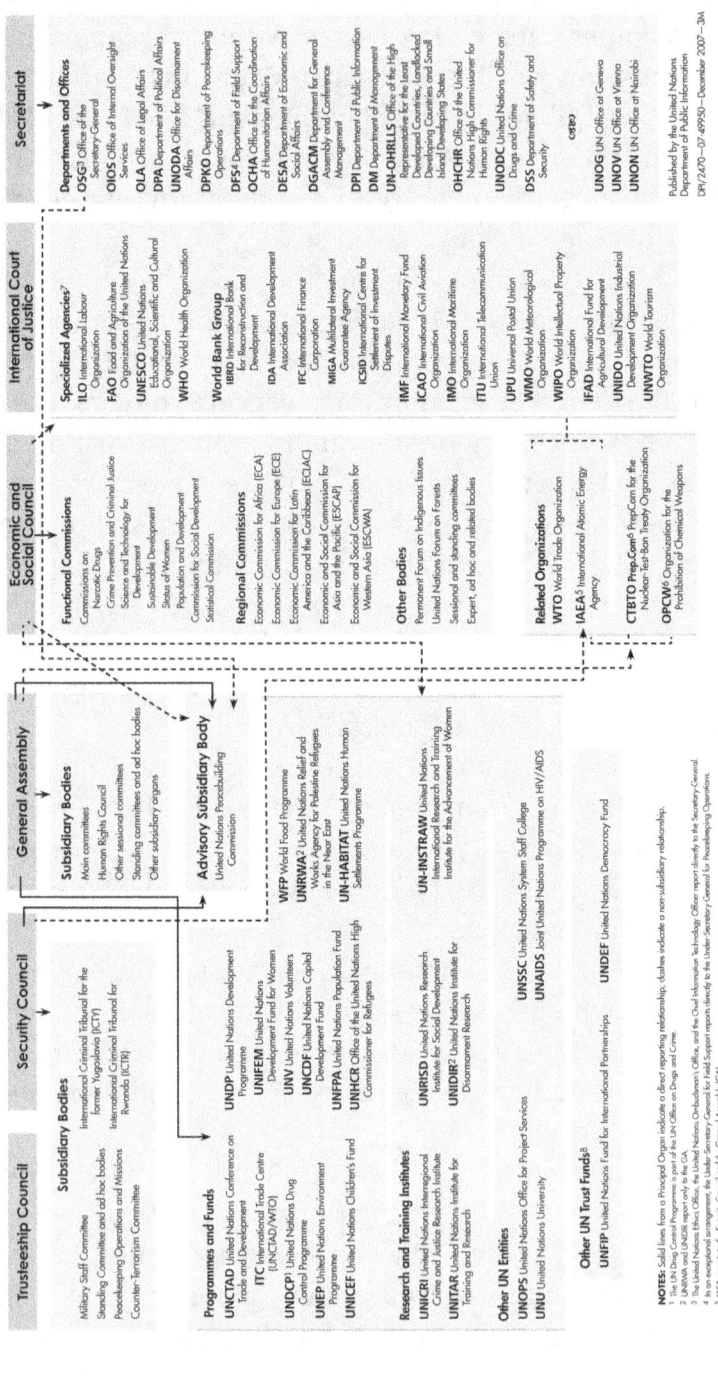

in due regard for the "necessity of securing the highest standards of efficiency, competence, and integrity" (Article 101).

Authors' Note: The chart on page 22 does not reflect the newly established United Nations Entity for Gender Equality and the Empowerment of Women — UN Women — established in January 2011.

Women at the United Nations

World Conference of the International Women's Year,
Mexico City, June 1975 / UN Photo, B. Lane

Women at the United Nations

"To this end, we call on the Governments of the world to encourage women everywhere to take a more active part in national and international affairs, and on women who are conscious of their opportunities to come forward and share in the work of peace and reconstruction as they did in war and resistance."

— Eleanor Roosevelt, addressing the inaugural meeting of the General Assembly as a US delegate in London, February 1946.

In January 2011, a newly established United Nations Entity for Gender Equality and the Empowerment of Women — UN Women — officially began its work. Headed by the former president of Chile, Michelle Bachelet, UN Women aims to accelerate progress toward gender equality and women's empowerment in the recognition that gender equality is not only a basic human right, but a prerequisite for development and sustained growth.

The creation of UN Women epitomizes the decades of work the UN has done to meet the needs of girls and women around the world. Since the organization was first established in 1945, issues of women have been at the forefront of its work. The UN Charter clearly reaffirms "the equal rights of men and women" (Preamble) and declares that one of the purposes of the organization is "[t]o achieve international co-operation...in promoting and encouraging respect for human rights and for fundamental freedoms for all without distinction as to race, sex, language, or religion." The charter also paves the way for both men and women "to participate in any capacity and under conditions of equality in [the UN's] principal and subsidiary organs" (Article 8).

About UN Women

In July 2010, the United Nations General Assembly created UN Women, the United Nations Entity for Gender Equality and the Empowerment of Women. In doing so, UN member states took an historic step in accelerating the organization's goals on gender equality and the empowerment of women. The creation of UN Women came about as part of the UN reform agenda, bringing together resources and mandates for greater impact. It merges and builds on the important work of four previously distinct parts of the UN system, which focused exclusively on gender equality and women's empowerment.
• Division for the Advancement of Women (DAW)
• International Research and Training Institute for the Advancement of Women (INSTRAW)
• Office of the Special Adviser on Gender Issues and Advancement of Women (OSAGI)
• United Nations Development Fund for Women (UNIFEM)

The main roles of UN Women are:
• To support inter-governmental bodies, such as the Commission on the Status of Women, in their formulation of policies, global standards, and norms.
• To help member states to implement these standards, standing ready to provide suitable technical and financial support to those countries that request it, and to forge effective partnerships with civil society.
• To hold the UN system accountable for its own commitments on gender equality, including regular monitoring of system-wide progress.

Source: Text taken from UN Women website: *http://www.unwomen.org/about-us/about-un-women/*

Throughout its history, the UN has established various bodies to promote and protect women's rights. Within its first year, ECOSOC established a Commission on the Status of Women (CSW) with the mandate "to prepare recommendations and reports to the Economic and Social Council on promoting women's rights in political, economic, civil, social, and educational fields."[1] The commission, which meets annually in UN headquarters, has grown into a preeminent global policymaking body on gender equality and the advancement of women. In order to provide secretariat functions to CSW, the UN also created a Section on the Status of Women at that time, which became the Division for the Advancement of Women in 1978.

The equal rights of women and men were formalized in the Universal Declaration of Human Rights of 1948, which declared that "[a]ll human beings are born free and equal in dignity and rights" and that "[e]veryone is entitled to all the rights and freedoms set forth in this Declaration, without distinction of any kind, such as race, colour, sex...."[2] This declaration signalled a fundamental shift to the use of gender-sensitive language in international documents, laying the groundwork for women to define and exercise their "rights"[3] in the international policymaking arena.

From 1947 to 1962, the UN concentrated its efforts on laying the legal foundations for gender equality by setting standards and formulating international conventions to change discriminatory legislation.[4] It also worked closely with nongovernmental organizations to foster global awareness and collect data on women's issues. One of the first conventions devoted exclusively to empowering women was the Convention on the Political Rights of Women, which the General Assembly adopted in 1952. This convention guarantees women the equal right to vote, run for election, and hold public office as men in all adhering countries. This was followed with the Convention on the Nationality of Married Women (1957), which protects women's rights to nationality regardless of their marriage to alien husbands, and the

Vijaya Lakshmi Pandit (1900–1990):
The First Woman President of the UN General Assembly

Daughter of an aristocratic nationalist leader and sister of Jawaharlal Nehru, the first prime minister of independent India, Pandit was an activist in the Indian nationalist movement and was imprisoned three times by British authorities. She entered municipal government in Allahabad (western India) before entering the legislative assembly of the United Provinces and becoming minister for local self-government and public health (1937–39), the first Indian woman to hold a cabinet postition.

With Indian independence, Pandit embarked on a distinguished diplomatic career, leading the Indian delegation to the UN (1946–48, 1952–53) and serving as India's ambassador to Moscow, Washington, Mexico, London, and Dublin. In 1953, Pandit became the first woman to be elected president of the UN General Assembly.

Upon returning to India, she served as governor of the state of Maharashtra and became a member of the Indian parliament, representing the constituency formerly represented by Jawaharlal Nehru (1964–1968). In 1978, she was appointed the Indian representative to the UN Human Rights Commission.

In an interview for the *United Nations Bulletin* in 1953, Pandit shared her philosophy: "Those of us who have been brought up under the shadow of Gandhi and trained under his leadership must inevitably approach international problems from his angle. It is for this reason that we are occasionally misunderstood. The great contribution that Mahatma Gandhi made was his insistence that means are as important as ends and that if the goal towards which we travel is a good one, we cannot employ means that are unworthy. In our own small way we attempt to apply this principle in our own work in the United Nations... The United Nations' existence depends on its ability to translate the noble words and high ideals of the Charter into the lives of the humblest individuals in the smallest nations."

Source: Encyclopedia Britannica Profile: 300 Women Who Changed the World, *www. britannica.com/women/article-9058241*; Jain, Devaki. *Women, Development, and the UN: A Sixty-year Quest for Equality and Justice* (Indiana University Press, 2005).

Convention on Consent to Marriage, Minimum Age for Marriage and Registration of Marriages (1962), which reaffirms the consensual nature of marriages. This convention also requires the parties to establish minimum age and to ensure the registration of marriages.

During this time, UN specialized agencies undertook specific initiatives to enhance women's economic and social opportunities around the world. In 1951, the International Labour Organization (ILO) established the Convention concerning Equal Remuneration for Men and Women Workers for Work of Equal Value, while the United Nations Educational, Scientific and Cultural Organization (UNESCO) developed programs to increase women's literacy and access to education in collaboration with CSW.[5] In 1960, UNESCO adopted the Convention against Discrimination in Education, to combat segregation and discrimination in the field of education.

The 1960s and 1970s saw profound changes in the United Nations, with its membership jumping from 82 in 1958 to 152 by 1979.[6] The new additions consisted mostly of newly independent countries whose major concerns pertained to poverty and development. The UN proclaimed 1960 to 1970 as the First Development Decade and systematically investigated for the first time the role of women in national development plans. CSW also researched socioeconomic status of women around the world. Studies undertaken during this period showed that women were "affected disproportionately by poverty and inequality with men — including barriers to women's ownership of land and access to credit," and prompted the General Assembly to adopt a Declaration on the Elimination of Discrimination against Women in 1967, "a watershed in the UN's quest for women's equality."[7] While there were also findings that women acted as "producers, as bread winners," especially in the former colonies, the United Nations' development agencies continued to view women primarily as "mothers, homemakers, and the 'frailer sex.'"[8]

During the second United Nations Decade for Development,

from 1970 to 1980, the world experienced a deepening awareness of discrimination against women and saw a rise in the number of organizations committed to women's causes. This trend was accompanied by increasing recognition that women played an important role in development, as argued in the seminal book *Women's Role in Economic Development* by Ester Boserup (1910–1999). Boutros Boutros-Ghali, the UN's sixth secretary-general (1992–1996), recalled that during this period, there was "a growing perception at the UN and elsewhere that the low status of women, especially in developing countries, was a major factor in such increasingly globalized problems as poverty, rapid population growth, illiteracy, malnutrition, migration and forced urbanization, and poor health conditions."[9]

In 1972, the UN launched wide-ranging efforts to integrate women's perspectives into development processes, including the appointment of a woman to head the Centre for Social Development and Humanitarian Affairs. Helvi Sipilä of Finland, who previously served as a special rapporteur for CSW's Status of Women and Family Planning Project, became the first woman to occupy the position of an assistant secretary-general. (At the time, 97 percent of the organization's senior management — director level and above – was male.)[10]

The same year, in celebration of its twenty-fifth anniversary, the CSW recommended designating 1975 as International Women's Year. The General Assembly subsequently adopted a resolution "to devote this year to intensified action to promote equality between men and women; to ensure the full integration of women in the total development effort...and to recognize the importance of women's increasing contribution to the development of friendly relations and co-operation among States."[11]

To observe the International Women's Year, the General Assembly decided to organize, at the recommendation of CSW, an international conference in Mexico City on the theme of equality, development, and peace. Attended by 133 government delegations and some 6,000 civil society representatives, the conference proved to be "the start of the most vibrant and influential phase of the worldwide women's movement."[12]

The conference adopted a comprehensive set of guidelines for the advancement of women — the World Plan of Action for the Implementation of the Objectives of the International Women's Year — and led the General Assembly to declare 1976 to 1985 the UN Decade for Women: Equality, Development and Peace. Designed to facilitate "effective and sustained national, regional, and international action to implement the World Plan of Action,"[13] the decade contributed to bringing legitimacy to the international women's movement and substantially elevated women's issues on the global agenda.[14] The decade also helped to shift the view from "development is good for women" to "development is not possible without women."[15]

The First World Conference on Women also led to the creation of the International Research and Training Institute for the Advancement of Women (INSTRAW) and the United Nations Development Fund for Women (UNIFEM). Based in Santo Domingo, Dominican Republic, INSTRAW's activities focused on integration of women in the development process, both as its participants and beneficiaries, through research, training, and the collection and dissemination of information. UNIFEM, which was originally set up as the Voluntary Fund for the Decade for Women, provided direct support to development projects for women in an attempt to improve their living standards.[i]

The momentum generated by the International Women's Year and the world conference in Mexico led, in 1979, to the adoption of the Convention on the Elimination of All Forms of Discrimination against Women (CEDAW),[ii] described as "an

---

i. UNIFEM became an autonomous body in association with the United Nations Development Programme (UNDP) in 1985. Both UNIFEM and INSTRAW were merged into the UN Entity for Gender Equality and the Empowerment of Women in January 2011.

ii. CEDAW was adopted by the General Assembly in 1979 by a vote of 130 international bill of rights for women."[16] The Convention grew out of the perception that the attempts to implement the Declaration on the Elimination of Discrimination against Women were limited due to its voluntary nature.[17] Containing effective implementation procedures, CEDAW defined discrimination against women as "any distinction, exclusion or restriction made on the basis of sex which has the effect or purpose of impairing or nullifying the recognition, enjoyment or exercise by women, irrespective of their marital status, on a basis of equality of men and women, of human rights and fundamental freedoms in the political, economic, social, cultural, civil or any other field" (Article 1). CEDAW effectively established the centrality of non-discrimination in promoting gender equality, and set up an agenda for national action to end discrimination.[18]

In July 1980, 145 UN member states gathered in Copenhagen for the Second World Conference on Women to review and accelerate the progress made towards the implementation of the World Plan of Action.[iii] By then, there was a clear understanding — as advanced by the Non-Aligned Movement (NAM)[iv]— of "the interconnection between trends in women's roles and status in their societies and the nature and pattern of the development processes, including the latter's dependence on international, economic, and political relations."[19] With this frame of mind, member states focused on providing women with equal access to education, employment opportunities, and healthcare services.[20]

In 1985, the Third World Conference on Women convened in Nairobi to review and appraise the achievements of the UN Decade for Women: Equality, Development and Peace. Its mandate

---

member states and 10 abstentions. It entered into force on 3 September 1981,
iii. In parallel with the Second World Conference, over 8,000 participants from 187 countries attended the NGO forum to discuss the major themes of the conference.
iv. The Non-Aligned Movement was formed in 1961 by a group of 25 states that were concerned about the accelerating arms race and were not aligned with either of the Cold War powers.

was to devise concrete ways of overcoming obstacles for achieving the objectives of the decade.[21] The conference concluded with the Nairobi Forward-looking Strategies for the Advancement of Women, which provided a comprehensive blueprint for the advancement of women and the elimination of gender-based discrimination for the period 1986 to 2000. The strategies also recommended strengthening the integration of women in the development process, and established three basic categories to measure the prospective progress: constitutional and legal measures, equality in social participation, and equality in political participation and decision-making.[22]

In the late 1980s and early 1990s, the Commission on the Status of Women, the CEDAW Committee, and the Commission on Human Rights began to highlight the issue of violence against women, which had been considered until then a "private" matter beyond the scope of public and human rights interventions.[23] Spurred on by nongovernmental organizations, the General Assembly adopted the Declaration for the Elimination of Violence against Women in December 1993. In the following year, the Commission on Human Rights appointed a special rapporteur on violence against women, its causes, and consequences (Radhika Coomaraswamy, 1994–2003) to recommend measures to eliminate violence throughout the world.

In 1995, the Fourth World Conference on Women: Action for Equality, Development and Peace took place in Beijing, marking a watershed event in the history of global women's empowerment. The conference came at a moment of "political maturity" on the part of the global women's movement, capable of accommodating differences and articulating clear goals and policies for the international community.[24] Attended by 6,000 delegates from 189 countries and more than 5,000 representatives from nongovernmental organizations, the conference also remains the largest UN conference to date. The Beijing Declaration and Platform for Action, the major outcomes of the conference, significantly

Milestones in the History of Gender Equality and Empowerment of Women

1946   Establishment of the Commission on the Status of Women
1948   Adoption of the Universal Declaration of Human Rights
1952   Adoption of the Convention on the Political Rights of Women
1957   Adoption of the Convention on the Nationality of Married Women
1962   Adoption of the Convention on Consent to Marriage, Minimum Age for Marriage and Registration of Marriages
1967   Declaration on the Elimination of Discrimination against Women
1975   International Women's Year
        First World Conference on Women (Mexico City)
1976–85 United Nations Decade for Women
1979   Adoption of the Convention on the Elimination of All Forms of Discrimination against Women
1980   Second World Conference on Women (Copenhagen)
1985   Third World Conference on Women (Nairobi)
1993   Declaration for the Elimination of Violence against Women
1995   Fourth World Conference on Women (Beijing)
2000   Adoption of the United Nations Millennium Declaration
2005   Ten-year review of the implementation of the Beijing Declaration and Platform for Action (New York)
        World Summit (New York)
2011   Establishment of the United Nations Entity for Gender Equality and the Empowerment of Women
        Centenary of International Women's Day (1911–2011)

advanced the global agenda for women's human rights and gender equality, and continue to inform the work of the UN on women.[v]

Five years after the Beijing conference, CSW organized a special session, Women 2000: Gender Equality, Development, and Peace for the Twenty-first Century in June, in which member states agreed on further actions to implement the Beijing Declaration and Platform for Action. More importantly, in September 2000, world leaders met in New York and adopted the UN Millennium Declaration, committing their nations to achieve, by 2015, eight overarching goals that have become known as the Millennium Development Goals (MDGs). The MDGs aim to make progress on poverty eradication, universal education, gender equality, child health, maternal health, HIV/AIDS, environmental sustainability, and global partnership for development. In particular, MDG3 to "promote gender equality and empower women" contains a specific target to eliminate gender disparity in all levels of education. MDG5 is also dedicated to women, striving to reduce maternity mortality rate, while achieving universal access to reproductive health.[25]

The decades of efforts toward enhancing the socioeconomic and political status of women culminated in the idea of "gender mainstreaming." This idea gained full momentum in Beijing when a consensus was reached that women must claim formal power to directly shape public policy.[26] In 1997, ECOSOC defined gender mainstreaming as:

> the process of assessing the implications for women and men of any planned action, including legislation, policies

v. The Platform for Action reflects the new international commitment to achieving the goals of equality, development, and peace for women, with the following critical areas of concern: 1) women and poverty, 2) education and training of women, 3) women and health, 4) violence against women, 5) women and armed conflict, 6) women and the economy, 7) women in power and decision-making, 8) institutional mechanisms for the advancement of women, 9) human rights of women, 10) women and the media, 11) women and the environment, and 12) the girl child.

and programmes, in all areas and at all levels, and as a strategy for making women's as well as men's concerns and experiences an integral dimension of the design, implementation, monitoring and evaluation of policies and programmes in all political, economic and social spheres so that women and men benefit equally and inequality is not perpetuated. The ultimate goal is to achieve gender equality. [27]

Since then, gender mainstreaming has become a pivotal part of the UN's work, from development and disaster risk reduction to peace and security. For example, in October 2000, the Security Council adopted resolution 1325 on women, peace, and security, which recognized the important role of women in peace building as well as gender dimensions of peace processes and conflict resolution.

The adoption of the Security Council resolution 1325 signalled the expanding role of women as development partners to promoters of peace and security. At the World Summit in 2005, world leaders "[stressed] the important role of women in the prevention and resolution of conflicts and in peace building."[28] This view arose from the recognition that women, like men, are both actors and victims in armed conflicts, who experience conflict differently than men and boys.[vi] In addition to suffering from gender-based and sexual violence, women and girls are particularly vulnerable to trafficking, forced labor, and detention. By making women active partners in the development of peace and security, the UN sought to "ensure that awareness of these violations informs planning and implementation in all peace support operations, humanitarian activities and reconstruction efforts."[29]

---

vi. Armed conflicts continue to occur in many parts of the world. In Africa, over one quarter of the continent's 53 countries were affected by conflict in the late 1990s. (Study submitted by the UN Secretary-General on Women, Peace and Security, 2002.)

Female senior managers with Secretary-General Ban Ki-moon,
December 2009 / UN Photo, Mark Garten

Creating a World Fit for Future Generations[vii]

The UN is now in the midst of its seventh decade. While the organization has made notable progress to realize gender equality and women's full empowerment, much remains to be done at the national, regional, and international levels by all stakeholders, including governments, civil society organizations, and the private sector.

The General Assembly's decision to establish the United Nations Entity for Gender Equality and the Empowerment of Women in July 2010 represents a positive step toward strengthening the institutional support for activities designed to benefit girls and women around the world.[viii] Further, the United Nations is currently

vii. In the 2005 World Summit in New York, world leaders reaffirmed that gender equality and the protection of all human rights and fundamental freedoms are essential to advancing development, peace, and security, and expressed their commitment to "creating a world fit for future generations, which takes into account the best interests of the child" (Summit outcome document, paragraph 12).

viii. UN Women's focus areas include violence against women, peace and security, leadership and participation, economic empowerment, national planning led by a secretary-general who has identified "women" as one of the key priorities for action.[ix] In addition to launching UNiTE to End Violence against Women (2008) and a campaign to combat maternal mortality (2010), Ban Ki-moon has appointed more female leaders at the helm of the organization than ever before.

In this context, the time is ripe for the UN and the international community as a whole to take concrete, ambitious steps to remove discrimination, educate and support girls, and give women the opportunity they deserve to fulfill their potential — and build on an international scale "[t]he true republic: men, their rights and nothing more; women, their rights and nothing less" (Susan B. Anthony, 1820–1906).

---

and budgeting, human rights, and the Millennium Development Goals.
ix. Secretary-General Ban Ki-moon's other priorities include climate change, disarmament, combating the financial crisis and poverty, global health, peace and security, responsibility to protect, and United Nations reform and account-ability.

Radhika Coomaraswamy

Uganda, June 2010

Staying True to Yourself

Radhika Coomaraswamy

In April 2006, former Secretary-General of the United Nations Kofi Annan appointed Ms. Radhika Coomaraswamy as Under-Secretary-General and Special Representative for Children and Armed Conflict. She was reappointed by Secretary-General Ban Ki-moon in February 2007.

The Special Representative for Children and Armed Conflict serves as an independent moral voice on behalf of children violated in situations of conflict around the world. The changing nature of conflict has dramatically increased the proportion of civilian casualties worldwide to more than 90 percent; half of these victims are children. According to the United Nations Children's Fund (UNICEF), an estimated 20 million children have been forced to flee their homes due to conflict and related human rights violations. More than two million children have died and an additional six million have been permanently disabled or seriously injured as a direct result of armed conflict in the last decade. Moreover, there are hundreds of thousands of children under the age of 18 involved in more than 30 conflicts. These children are continually exposed to life-threatening situations and experience painful emotional and psychological repercussions.

In this context, Radhika's mission is "to promote and protect the rights of all children affected by armed conflict" by working closely with governments, UN bodies, civil society groups, and other stakeholders. In particular, she stresses the importance of closely engaging national governments to ensure that the UN can more effectively support the efforts of national institutions in the protection, reintegration, and rehabilitation of children.

Six objectives drive the work of her office: 1) supporting global initiatives to end grave violations against children affected by conflict, including programs to monitor violations and end impunity for perpetrators; 2) promoting rights-based protection for affected children; 3) integrating children's concerns—such as their protection and demobilization from combatant forces—into UN peacekeeping and peace-building operations; 4) identifying new trends and strategies for the protection of children through research; 5) securing political engagement; and 6) raising global awareness on different aspects of children and armed conflict, from trafficking to psychological recovery and disruption of education.

The wide-ranging scope and highly emotional nature of her work—which involves advocating for close to 10,000 children that are killed or maimed by landmines each year—challenge Radhika to maintain a multifaceted yet philosophical perspective, wherein she can confidently declare, "I have all of the world's children to look after."

Ms. Coomaraswamy elegantly takes her seat for our interview. She is wearing all black with a violet shawl draped across her shoulders. She speaks in a velvety voice; her presence is calm, strong, and focused. Upon meeting her, one senses that her watchful presence is one to be respected.

From East to West and Back Again

Radhika Coomaraswamy was born in 1953 in Sri Lanka to a family of politically active and social-minded intellectuals. Her parents were strongly influenced and inspired by Mahatma Gandhi (1869–1948). His values, such as commitment to truth, civil rights, freedom, and nonviolence, contributed significantly to the formation of her parents' political consciousness, which in turn deeply affected the impressionable young minds of Radhika and her older brother.

Radhika's father was educated at the prestigious Oxford University in England and had worked for the UN as an assistant administrator in charge of Asia and the Pacific for the United Nations Development Programme (UNDP). "He was part of a generation of South Asians who were rooted both in South Asia and the wider international community at the same time," she says. Radhika's father wanted his children to follow in his footsteps and become "as cosmopolitan and aware of the world as he was."

Perhaps his exhortation was not necessary, as Radhika and her brother were destined to live international and culturally diverse lives as "children of the UN." When Radhika was seven, her father was posted to New York and the family left Sri Lanka for the Big Apple. Her mother, traditional and conservative, was content to defer to her husband's career—her life choice could not have been more different from Radhika's eventual path.

The two children attended the United Nations International School (UNIS), where social awareness and global outlook became part of their growth process. Founded in 1947 by a group of UN parents who wanted to provide international education while preserving diverse cultural heritage, the school offers "a global curriculum that inspires in its students the spirit and ideals of the United Nations Charter."[1] At the UNIS, before learning any national anthem, Radhika learned a "UN anthem"[i] about nations rising and uniting.

As a young girl, Radhika wanted to become a doctor. After focusing on biology and chemistry in high school, she was accepted to Yale University, where she intended to undertake pre-med studies. Although acceptance to Yale University—one of the best Ivy League schools in the US—is traditionally welcomed by one's family with open arms and praise, Radhika's experience was

---

i. Although many songs have been written about the UN and its work, there is no official anthem or hymn for the organization.

a bit different. "Some of my aunts were so disappointed when I enrolled in Yale, because they thought I should be getting married and having babies. To them, going to Yale meant that I would never do that. After all, they were very culturally conservative."

This is interesting to note, given that Sri Lanka has had a historical pattern of late marriages and widespread access to education for women. For example, in the early part of the twentieth century, Sri Lankan women were marrying, on the average, at 20 and 21 years of age, while their counterparts in neighboring India and Bangladesh were marrying at 13 years of age, on average.[2] By the early 1990s, Sri Lankan women were marrying at 25, while those in India were marrying at 20 and in Thailand at 23. The fact that Radhika's aunts, who came mostly from wealthy families, "scorned" her Yale education in favor of marriage seems to support ethnographic evidence that, historically, upper classes in Sri Lanka have a tradition of earlier marriages because of the importance attached to alliances, status, and the sexual purity of women.[3]

Despite being labeled "eccentric" by her aunts, Radhika joined the Yale Class of 1974 and became part of the second cohort of women to be admitted to the university.[ii] She was also the only South Asian woman in the entire undergraduate school. Her deepened self-awareness as an Asian woman notwithstanding, she never felt an outsider. She had "lovely" roommates, many of whom remain her close friends to this day, and she was surrounded by open-minded peers who embraced diversity and experimented with new thoughts. "It was a very exciting time for me," she says. Although the university itself was couched in a privileged setting, campus life still exposed her to various social ills of the day, such as poverty, racial prejudice, and gender discrimination, which gradually shifted her interest from medicine to public law and policy.

---

ii. Yale University allowed women to study in graduate programs as early as 1876, at the Yale Graduate School of Arts and Sciences. Admission of female undergraduate students began only in 1969, for the class of 1973.

On the whole, Radhika found her college experience positive and transformative, but she regrets that she did not "study hard enough." Intent on absorbing the world rather than the books, she preferred to debate social issues with her friends than bury herself in theories. Moreover, since she was a pre-med student, her curricula in the first year consisted mostly of math and science with only a few "required" courses in the humanities and social sciences. In her second year, she shifted to the humanities, but today she feels that she did not make full use of her opportunities at Yale. She realized that she missed the once-in-a-lifetime chance to learn about different fields and expand her horizon. "If I could have done one thing different, I would definitely have taken advantage of my college years and learned as much as possible— literature, history, political science, what have you."

One of the most challenging aspects of her years at Yale was not having a role model who could provide guidance as to what path she should take. As the first South Asian woman on campus, Radhika essentially had to pioneer being a successful female South Asian student and set an example for other girls to follow.[iii] However, unlike other Asian Americans who retained a strong Asian identity, Radhika felt equally at home as an Asian and an American. She explained that she always straddled the two worlds, with one foot in the East and the other in the West. This may have been an effect of her years at the UN International School, where race was never a factor in her interactions with teachers and other students. There, as at home, she was encouraged to be a global-minded "Radhika" more than a Sri Lankan or an American girl.

That does not mean that she was not aware of her gender or ethnicity. She was fully aware of her unique endowments and

iii. In fact, it was not until the early 1970s that Asian American organizations were established to address issues of concern to their community. In particular, the 1978 Supreme Court decision on the Regents of the University of California versus Bakke, which ruled against the use of a racial quota system and "reverse discrimination," catalyzed the founding of major Asian student associations.

struggled to understand the limits and possibilities offered by these endowments. Without a role model, everything was up to Radhika to test and figure out. This quest would remain part of her life-long development process. She observes, "Life should be a constant identity crisis. You should be constantly challenged and constantly changing." The identity crisis referred to here is not a generic effort to understand oneself vis-à-vis the outside world but an effort to examine how best one can grow as an individual capable of making positive contributions to the world. For Radhika, identity crisis therefore meant rigorous SWOT analysis, identifying her strengths and weaknesses in the context of emerging opportunities and threats.

Early on in Radhika's pre-med studies at Yale, big changes were beginning to take shape in the island nation of Sri Lanka, which was called Ceylon until 1972. Sri Lanka gained independence from the British in 1948, after being subject to various colonial powers since 1505, when Portuguese traders first seized the island's coastal areas. Sri Lanka's post-independence politics has been strongly democratic, with two major parties—the United National Party (UNP) and the Sri Lanka Freedom Party (SLFP)—taking turns in power.

A major political upheaval occurred in 1971 when an insurrection rose against the then-ruling Sri Lankan Freedom Party (SLFP), which was headed by Sirimavo Bandaranaike, a widow of former Prime Minister Solomon Bandaranaike and the world's first female head of government.[iv] Bandaranaike acted swiftly to suppress the insurgents and declared a state of emergency that lasted six years. In 1972, her government adopted a new constitution that changed the name of the country from Ceylon to Sri Lanka and declared itself a republic instead of a Commonwealth realm nominally subject to the British crown. The

iv. Sirimavo Bandaranaike's husband was assassinated while in office as prime minister in 1959 and, as his successor, she became the world's first female head of government. Bandaranaike left office in 1965 and was elected back to office in 1970.

constitution also created a weak president appointed by the prime minister and made protection of Buddhism mandatory.

Simmering under these changes was the growing tension between the Sinhalese majority and the Tamil minority. Predominantly Buddhists, the Sinhalese are Indo-Aryans and constitute 74 percent of Sri Lanka's 21 million people. Tamils, on the other hand, are mostly Hindus and make up 18 percent of the population.[v]

After independence, Sri Lanka took aggressive measures to institute a Sinhalese-driven society. For example, in 1956, the government enacted the Official Language Act—also known as the Sinhala Only Act—to designate Sinhala, the language of the Sinhalese, as the sole official language of Sri Lanka. This happened right after Solomon Bandaranaike, Sirimavo's assassinated husband, swept into office on appeals to Sinhalese nationalism. The new language requirement effectively forced many Tamils out of civil service and, combined with discriminatory educational and agricultural policies, further aggravated the existing national divide. Tamils became increasingly radicalized such that by the mid-1970s, Tamil politicians who once supported federalism began to demand a separate Tamil state—Tamil Eelam—in northern and eastern Sri Lanka, which has traditionally been inhabited by Tamils. Decades of intermittent violence between the Sinhalese government and the separatist militant organization, the Liberation Tigers of Tamil Eelam, which used ruthless terrorist methods, erupted into a full-blown civil war in 1983, which killed and displaced thousands of Tamils over the next two decades.[vi]

Radhika came of age while all these changes were taking place in her birth country. Closer to Yale, she was also witnessing how law was being used to implement social change and justice, especially in terms of gender equality. Profoundly influenced by the interplay

---

v. Other minorities include Muslims (seven percent of the population) and Burghers, who are descendants of European colonists.
vi. The civil war officially ended on May 19, 2009, with the defeat of the Liberation Tigers of Tamil Eelam.

of law, politics, and society, Radhika gave up her aspirations to become a doctor and turned her attention to public-interest law. She was subsequently accepted to Columbia Law School in New York and spent three years there, becoming actively involved in international human rights law.[vii]

After receiving a juris doctor degree, Radhika had a choice between two career opportunities. The first was to work for a prestigious law firm in the US, and the second was to return to Sri Lanka, where the tension between the two ethnic groups was intensifying. As a minority Tamil, she felt strongly connected to the events unfolding in her home country and felt an urge to contribute to building a more peaceful and just society. "Sri Lanka was going through major turmoil, but there was great potential for change. My family had instilled a strong sense of service in me and my brother, and I never felt that there was any other option but to go back. My brother also chose to return to Sri Lanka at that time." Fortunately, there was a position open at the Marga Institute,[viii] a newly established independent think tank whose mission of achieving just and equitable development in Sri Lanka aligned exactly with Radhika's interests and priorities. Radhika joined the institute without hesitation.

Becoming a Woman Activist

Returning to Sri Lanka was a reverse culture shock. Radhika was used to leading an autonomous life in the US, where she openly shared her views and lived her life as a free and independent woman. Back in Sri Lanka, she had more expectations to conform

vii. Radhika later received a master of laws (LLM) from Harvard University and honorary PhDs from Amherst College, the Katholieke Universiteit Leuven, the University of Edinburgh, and the University of Essex.
viii. Established in April 1972 by a group of Sri Lankan government officials, academics, and professionals, the Marga Institute seeks to contribute to a just and equitable development process in Sri Lanka through multi-disciplinary research and national dialogue on development issues.

Sudan, January 2007

to, both from her extended family and from the wider community. Radhika remembers that she had to "negotiate" her adjustment into Sri Lankan society, which, despite being relatively progressive with respect to women's rights, continued to cast women as "the reproducers, nurturers, and disseminators of 'tradition,' 'culture,' 'community,' and 'nation.'"[4] As a single, "overeducated" woman, Radhika found herself in a unique situation, where she was expected not only to marry and "reproduce" but also to make substantial contributions to the country's development efforts.

Despite the shock of her new cultural surroundings and, in some cases, boundaries, Radhika remembers this time as being one of the most exciting in her career. Here she met an "extraordinary mentor," Kumari Jayawardena. Born in 1931, Kumari was then teaching political science at the University of Colombo and championing feminist issues that were indigenous to Sri Lanka and other third world countries. Although Kumari was Sinhalese, she took Radhika under her wing and introduced her to the world of academics, women's rights, and peace movements. They often joined Muslim women and traveled around the country and across

Asia, speaking about combating racism and achieving peace. It was during this time that Radhika saw firsthand shocking cases of abuse and violence against women and further resolved to fight for women's causes.

Radhika also met Neelan Tiruchelvam (1944–1999),[ix] "a scholar, an activist, and a visionary" from Sri Lanka, who advocated for the realization of peace, human rights, democracy, and pluralism through scholarship, activism, and politics. Describing him as "my mentor and my guide," Radhika explains that his emphasis on social dialogue, consensus building, and tolerance greatly affected her worldview as well as her approach to solving problems throughout her career. According to Radhika, it is important for young people to surround themselves with those whose ideals and actions they can respect and learn from, "for greatness is best inspired by a fellow human being in action."

Like-minded colleagues and mentors like Kumari and Neelan sustained Radhika during her time of struggle for social justice and women's rights in Sri Lanka. "The civil society actors were very dynamic, and even though we were in the minority, we gave each other the strength to continue fighting for what we believed in."

Standing up to the government as a Tamil and a female activist was certainly no easy feat, and Radhika was regularly and publicly attacked by her opponents. "Although I welcome constructive criticism in my current position and use it to improve my work, it was truly difficult to deal with the unwarranted personal attacks and criticism that I received at that time." Radhika quickly learned to develop a "thick skin."

Her work on behalf of women in Sri Lanka and the wider Asian region was recognized by the international community,

ix. Neelan Tiruchelvam was a Sri Lankan Tamil politician and an internationally renowned scholar who was assassinated by a Liberation Tigers of Tamil Eelam suicide bomber in 1999. He founded and directed the International Centre for Ethnic Studies and the Law and Society Trust, the country's leading research and policy organization.

and Radhika was appointed as the UN Special Rapporteur on Violence against Women in 1994. Special rapporteurs carry out "special procedures" established by the UN Human Rights Council (formerly the UN Commission on Human Rights) to address either specific country situations or thematic issues in all parts of the world.[x] These procedures are carried out either through an individual—called a special rapporteur, a special representative of the secretary-general, or an independent expert—or through a working group of usually five members, one from the UN's five regional groups: Africa, Asia, Eastern Europe, Latin America and the Caribbean, and Western Europe and Others. The mandate holders, who serve without pay in their personal capacity, examine, monitor, report, and advise on human rights situations of a specific country or thematic issue, such as adequate housing, torture, and human trafficking.

Radhika served as the UN Special Rapporteur on Violence against Women for ten years, from 1994 to 2003. During this time, she traveled the world, bearing witness to unspeakable atrocities, and spoke on behalf of women who were experiencing violence in their families, communities, and during armed conflict.

Urging governments to intervene more actively, Radhika frequently referred to the UN Declaration on the Elimination of Violence against Women, which reads, "States should condemn violence against women and should not invoke any custom, tradition, or religious consideration to avoid their obligations with respect to its elimination" (Article 4). Radhika also pioneered the idea of harnessing women's potential to contribute to the peace process. Noting that "those who give birth are averse to having life taken away," Radhika believed that women peacemakers provide "an alternative, more inclusive, way to resolve conflict." She urged

---

x. There are currently 31 thematic and eight country mandates (Burundi, Cambodia, North Korea, Haiti, Myanmar, occupied Palestine territories, Somalia, and Sudan). The UN Office of the High Commissioner for Human Rights provides these "special procedures" with personnel, policy, research, and logistical support.

governments "to involve women in the peace process, to ensure that voices of nurture and care are given a place at the negotiating table."[5]

As much as Radhika's work touched the lives of countless women around the world, she was equally touched by their strength and resilience. "I have met women in Rwanda who had been raped countless times in the most horrific ways, women trafficked in Eastern Europe, victims of domestic violence in Brazil. Despite having experienced such horror, somehow, many of them managed to emerge resilient and hopeful. That kind of human resilience inspires me. Those women inspire me."

At the same time, Radhika admits that the stories of some violated women "haunt" her, and intimates the emotionally and psychologically draining nature of her work. One example she gave was about a girl named Eva in the Eastern Congo. "On her way to school one day, she was waylaid by some young men with guns. She was taken to a camp, forced to remain nude, raped at will by the gang members, and also made to do domestic chores. She soon realized that her body had changed and that she was pregnant. She ran away from the camp, but the villagers were too afraid to help her. She finally jumped into a vehicle on the main highway and the driver took her to Panzi Hospital where she had her baby. Her large, sad eyes, filled with resignation, continue to haunt me. She was only 13 years old."[6]

In May 2003, Radhika was appointed the Chairperson of the Human Rights Commission of Sri Lanka,[xi] which was created in 1996 "to ensure human rights for all and to promote and protect the rule of law."[7] She was the third chairperson and the first woman to head the commission. As soon as Radhika took office, she drafted a strategic plan for the next three years, with a view to strengthen the

---

xi. The Human Rights Commission of Sri Lanka replaced two different institutions, which were promulgated under emergency regulations: the Human Rights Task Force to prevent illegal arrest and detention and the Commission for Eliminating Discrimination and Monitoring of Human Rights to prevent discrimination.

Human Rights Commission and improve the conditions of human rights in Sri Lanka. Four goals guided her work: 1) achieving stronger institutions, procedures, and awareness for human rights protection; 2) enhancing public awareness of their fundamental human rights; 3) developing the commission into an efficient and effective organization; and 4) reaching a final resolution of the post-civil war peace process. In recognition of her hard work on human rights and service to the country, the president of Sri Lanka conferred on Radhika the honorary title of Deshamanya (literally translated as "Pride of Nation") in 2007.[xii]

The World's Children to Look After

In April 2006, Radhika was appointed the Special Representative for Children and Armed Conflict at the UN. She moved back to New York to begin what would prove to be an immensely rewarding, exciting, and challenging opportunity. She was clear about the skill set that she brought to the "small office with very large goals." In addition to her varied expertise as a specialist on women and children's rights, she pointed out that her own experience in Sri Lanka, which has seen violent ethnic division and subsequent efforts at reintegration, has proven useful in dealing with the challenge of reintegrating former child soldiers and rape victims into society. Radhika also mentioned that her training as an academic enabled her to have a theoretical understanding of the issues at hand and to identify and fill research gaps, such as on the particular problems faced by girls in an armed conflict.

Much of her work builds on what Radhika calls the "landmark" UN Security Council resolution 1612, adopted in July 2005, which strongly condemns the recruitment and use of child soldiers and other violations and abuses committed against children in situations of conflict. The resolution requires the secretary-

---

xii. Deshamanya is the second-highest civil honor in Sri Lanka awarded by the government. It is used as a title or prefix to the recipient's name.

general to set up a monitoring and reporting mechanism to be operated in cooperation with national governments, relevant UN entities, and civil society organizations. Under this mandate, Radhika's office presents the findings of the monitoring process to the working group of the Security Council, which then makes recommendations on possible measures to promote the protection of children affected by armed conflict.

Monitoring children in precarious situations exposes Radhika to the horrific reality of what she and the rest of the international community are up against. In one of her public lectures in 2009, she told the story of Moi, a young Ugandan boy. "He was playing with his friend when guerrilla rebels attacked his village. He was abducted with his friend and made to carry loot from their village. On the way to the rebel camp, his friend fell and broke his ankle. The commander of the group shot his friend in the head. Moi was taken to camp, beaten, drugged, and trained to be a child soldier. He was made to attack his own village and kill and steal from family and friends."[8]

Ruthless commanders like this will do anything to use children because of the latter's susceptibility to brainwashing and vulnerability to physical force. With a bit of beating and drugging, any child can easily be turned into a fearless, robotic soldier. Other commanders, however, are more principled, and will not recruit child soldiers under any circumstances. Still others belong to an "ambiguous group" that accepts children who either volunteer or are sent by their parents or guardians.

Negotiation to release child soldiers is most productive with commanders who fall in the "ambiguous" range of moral strength. Often they do not have the strength to say no to children delivered directly into their camps. They also lack awareness about war crime consequences. Radhika provided an example of a satisfactory negotiation from the Central African Republic, where she met with Commandant Laurent Djim Wei of the Popular Army for the Restoration of Democracy (APRD). Facilitated by UN agencies that had already been in contact with the army for humanitarian activities, Radhika drove two hours into the bush to meet him. As expected, he was "initially a bit aggressive and defensive," but when she explained the problems of child soldiering and remedies available, the commandant showed willingness to consider releasing the children if there was a viable plan to take care of them, for these children "kept coming to him" because they were orphans.[9]

When asked which mission was most difficult for Radhika, she answers, "All missions are difficult in different ways." This is especially true because most of her field missions involve visiting places that have recently emerged from armed conflict, in which "the villages and cities resemble ghost towns with destroyed buildings, burnt livelihoods, and traumatized people."[10] Although the scale and extent of violations against children may differ from one place to another, each inevitably involves lives destroyed and dreams shattered. With such "human faces" attached to each mission, she finds it impossible to say that going to Gaza is more difficult than going to Sudan, for example. However, she observes that the Lord's Resistance Army in Uganda (LRA) is particularly "ruthless and determined to have children"[11] and, therefore, supports their indictment by the International Criminal Court rather than attempting to negotiate with them.

Looking Forward and Lessons Learned

Radhika's internationally recognized work on gender and human rights issues has affected the lives of countless vulnerable people around the world by drawing attention to their plights and initiating changes on a government level. When asked if there is anything that she would have done differently in her career (if, for instance, it would have been nice to take that first job with the law firm), Radhika smiles quietly and answers simply, "No. I am very happy with where I am right now. I have no regrets." She recalls with awe how every time she is just about to become burned out by what she is doing, she gets another call for a new commitment that inspires her all over again.

After retirement—although she has no plans for that anytime soon—Radhika hopes to return to the world of writing and academia. Having already published several books and articles on constitutional law, ethnic studies, and the status of women, she hopes to continue this work and do some more teaching, both in Sri Lanka and in the US.[xiii] Radhika never married and has no children. In addition to the pressures she has faced politically, she has also felt the societal pressure from her aunts and others to "settle down" and get married. In response to these societal expectations for having a family, she observes, "Maybe I just never met the right person. In any case, I believe I have the world's children to look after."

In addition to the world's children, Radhika also has two lovely nephews who have already agreed to one day take care of her when she reaches old age—a gift from her older brother, who now lives in London. He also works in international civil service as an economist for the Commonwealth of Nations, a voluntary association of 54 countries (most of which were formerly part of the British Empire) that cooperate on issues related to democracy and development.

Reflecting on her current position and the path that has taken her there, Radhika says that she feels "happy and fulfilled" and "hopes it will continue on this way." She plans to keep working in the international political arena for many years to come as she feels there is still much work to do. "In the post-WWII world there was so much idealism and excitement about what the world could be. Now there is a climate of fear, hatred, and cynicism. What we need is to work toward a culture of peace, even as we meet the

---

xiii. Radhika is currently a member of the global faculty at the New York University School of Law and teaches a summer course at the New College in Oxford University every July.

Myanmar, June 2007

terrible challenges in a hostile world."

Radhika describes how part of her vision is to see the international civil service become even more gender-balanced than it is today. She believes that although there is still an element of politics involved, it is important to uphold the UN Charter by developing and hiring a certain cadre of people to carry out the organization's missions. This cadre of people must represent the full diversity of the people the UN serves, in terms of national origin, ethnicity, and gender.

In 2006, there were just two women at the senior management level at the UN; today, the secretariat has been transformed with the appointment of multiple women to under-secretary-general positions. "Many UN staff feel that there are still obstacles to reaching senior management positions, especially for women. For instance, the dual burden that many face—having to balance work and family—can make career development very difficult." In addition to this dual burden, she notes that although structural changes have been made, there are still underlying attitudes that make it difficult for women at the UN. Never the one to shy away from confronting the truth, she says, "[T]here is still a tendency among some of the older male directors to not value women's work and opinions as much as men's." These attitudes must change before we can have the type of UN that would best serve all of the world's people.

When asked what it takes to be successful in a position of power, Radhika thoughtfully replies, "You must be able to inspire… you must have a vision of what you want to achieve and how you will achieve it. In order to achieve these things, you must also be able to make difficult choices." Important to achieving one's vision is having the emotional intelligence—the personal and social skills—necessary to encourage people to work together even when times are difficult.

As a person in a position of power at the UN, one must also have passion for social work. Radhika believes that this is "absolutely essential." From her experiences working with women and children in desperate situations throughout the globe, Radhika still believes in the fundamental goodness of the human spirit. "I think that everyone is born with compassion," she says pointedly, "but they are hardened by life's experiences." The key to successful social work is to create an enabling environment for the "goodness of the human spirit" to revive and prevail.

Radhika's unwavering compassion and commitment to human rights for all people have been recognized by many organizations across the globe. Although she is humbled by the honor of the title Deshamanya (not to mention shocked, as she admits that she spent much of her career criticizing the Sri Lankan government to do more for human rights), it is clear that Radhika believes in placing less value on outward recognition and more on one's inner integrity. In addition to the title of Deshamanya, Radhika has received countless other awards for her work, including the International Law Award from the American Bar Association, the Human Rights Award from the International Human Rights Law Group, the Bruno Kreisky Award of 2000, and honors from major universities around the world.

Middle East, April 2007

Although Radhika finds peace and fulfillment through focusing on career, she does not believe that everyone must follow suit. "Not everyone needs to be a high-powered woman," she says firmly. "Success depends on what you want to be, whether that's an artist or a lawyer or a mother. The most important thing is to be true to yourself and your dreams." She adds, "I strongly believe that if you get your energy from that, everything else falls into place sooner or later. If you know what you want and follow your dream, it is easier. The pitfalls are that anywhere in the world, any workplace, there are negative forces, such as people that are too bureaucratic, who may be too competitive; the clue to success is never let yourself be trapped by the negative forces. Everybody should try to rise above them and continue with their own personal tasks. To avoid negative waves, keep track of your positive logic."[12]

Radhika confides that she has been able to stay true to herself in her many dealings with opposing forces throughout her life by focusing on the values that matter most to her. Above all, Radhika hopes to be remembered as "someone who spoke truth to power." Throughout her distinguished career, she has had the opportunity to speak on behalf of those unable to speak for themselves, to speak truth to power, while also having compassion for the weak and vulnerable.

Staying True to Yourself

Radhika shows us that no one else can define who you are and that your inner strength is a thing of great value and importance. Developing a thick skin was a requirement for a woman such as herself, living in a world that was not always quick to accept her point of view or her choices in life. Through it all, through constantly growing and balancing multiple perspectives as a truly global citizen, she managed to stay true to exactly who she is.

Angela Kane

Eritrea, 2004

Being a Woman

Angela Kane

On May 13, 2008, United Nations Secretary-General Ban Ki-moon announced the appointment of Ms. Angela Kane as Under-Secretary-General for Management. The Under-Secretary-General for Management is responsible for heading the Department of Management, which provides services to support the day-to-day operations of the global UN Secretariat, which has some 44,000 staff members and a regular program budget of US $5.156 billion (for the 2010–2011 biennium).[1] The department's mission is "to formulate policies and procedures and provide strategic guidance, direction, and support in three broad management areas: human resources, finance and budget, and central support services."[2] It also oversees the renovation of the headquarters of the UN in New York, a massive project called the Capital Master Plan.[i]

As an administrative arm of the secretary-general, the Department of Management spearheads key initiatives to support his reform agenda. Although reform has always been a part of the UN's institutional history, it has received heightened attention since Ban Ki-moon took office in January 2007. In a separate UN website dedicated to reform, he declares, "Seldom has the UN been called upon to do so much for so many. I am determined to breathe new life and inject renewed confidence into a strengthened UN

---

i. The Capital Master Plan manages the historic renovation of the UN headquarters complex in New York City, which was built between 1949 and 1952. A five-year project (2008 to 2013) with a US $1.87 billion budget, the renovation aims to result in a safer and more energy-efficient UN complex.

firmly anchored in the twenty-first century, and which is effective, efficient, coherent, and accountable."[3] To advance this vision for a strengthened organization, the Department of Management puts its priority on working with relevant UN bodies to implement reform in human resources management, procurement, accountability, accounting standards, and enterprise resource planning.

> *Ms. Kane has just ended a meeting with the budget committee of the UN's internal management team. A group of mostly male officials in dark suits files out of her office into the waiting area. As we first glimpse Ms. Kane, she is bright-eyed and impeccably dressed in a stunning red skirt suit that would surely stand out in any male-dominated meeting. This conscious choice gives an impression of her poise and confidence as an efficient female manager.*

A German English Major

"I remember there was one local woman who had gotten a divorce, and it was quite a scandal. *Everyone* knew who she was. The criticism eventually got to be too much for her, and she had to move away from our town." Angela was born in 1948 in Hameln, Lower Saxony, Germany. In the 1950s, the town of Hameln was very small and homogenous. The next town over, Hannover, had 500,000 people. "We all considered it a very big excursion to go to Hannover, but really, it was only an hour away by car," Angela says, amused, offering insight into the small-town life and perspective of her hometown. Such a small town, where everyone knew each other's personal business, seems an unlikely setting for the coming of age of such a cosmopolitan and global-minded woman as Angela. The poignant memory of a divorced woman from her childhood speaks volumes about the societal restrictions placed on women while she was growing up.

Angela's family was hardworking and very supportive in terms of her education. As was typical during the time, Angela's mother married young and never worked outside the home. Despite her own limited education and lack of a professional life, Angela's mother often told her how important it was to get an education. An education, she repeated, was one thing that no one could take away from you—a theme common throughout the stories of all of the women we profiled. A strong education and encouragement can take a girl far.

As for Angela's father, he had been drafted into World War II immediately after high school, going on to serve in the German military for seven years. As the war had wreaked havoc on the overall German economy, there was little disposable income amongst the majority of the population. Like many Germans at the time, Angela's parents lacked the means to travel, and Angela grew up longing to see the world.

Angela got her first taste of "seeing the world" when she made the decision at age 12 (with permission from her parents, of course) to go away to a month-long summer camp organized by a local church. Away from home for the first time, she was terribly homesick but quickly taught herself to cope. After all, she reasoned, it was her decision to leave home, and she would have to accept the consequences of her decision. Dealing with some discomfort was worth it if she ever wanted to reap the benefits of doing new things and seeing new places. This strength of resolve would serve her well in many difficult experiences in her life — experiences that, once overcome, resulted in a great sense of achievement.

True to what her mother had hoped, Angela was a bright and dedicated student who maintained excellent grades throughout her schooling. When it came time for her to go away to university in 1967, Angela chose the University of Munich (Ludwig-Maximilians-Universität München); it was her first chance to live in a big city. At the time, West Germany was swept up in student protests against the perceived authoritarianism and hypocrisy of the German government. Fueled by contemporary international movements, students launched sit-ins, disruption of lectures, and attacks against major publishing companies to demand democracy, social justice, university reform, and an end to the Vietnam War. In particular, students wanted a complete closure to the German chapter of fascist rule by expelling professors and government officials with Nazi ties.

It was a breathtaking time. "My first year at the university was really incredible, socially, because of all of the exciting changes happening, but the downside is that it was very difficult to focus academically. I felt that I needed to move on if I was going to study seriously." Angela was unsure of how to shape her academic experience into the one that she envisioned for herself until an American friend at the university suggested that she consider going to college in the US; it would give her an opportunity to polish her English skills and live abroad for the first time — a win-win situation for Angela. After careful consideration, Angela took the SATs and the following year enrolled in the prestigious Bryn Mawr College, an elite all-girls college in Pennsylvania, with a full scholarship.

Once at Bryn Mawr, Angela had little trouble adjusting to the social environment, as she had attended an all-girls high school in Germany; however, keeping up with her English-language class posed a huge challenge in the beginning. Moreover, there were only a handful of foreign students on the campus, and she often felt isolated. Even though it was difficult and lonely at times, Angela's resolve pushed her to stick with it. After all, it was her decision to go to Bryn Mawr, and she had to live with it.

"They practically laughed at me when I said I wanted to major in English. How can a foreigner major in English? So, I acquiesced and decided to major in French, instead." To her further dismay and frustration, Angela was also informed that she would need to enroll as a freshman, even though she had already completed a year of university in Munich. As Angela describes her experience at Bryn Mawr, she exudes sharpness and wit that let us know that

*Addressing Indian troops as Deputy Special Representative for the
UN peacekeeping mission in Ethiopia and Eritrea, 2004*

this seeming "setback" did not get the best of her. In the end, after a bit of negotiation, a bit of coercion, and plenty of hard work, Angela was able to graduate in just two years. "And they offered that I major in English," she adds.

Going Global

"What do you do with a language major?" she asks ironically, smiling. Upon graduation from Bryn Mawr, Angela briefly went back to Germany to reevaluate her career prospects. Soon after, she returned to the US to explore her options. While in the US, Angela stayed with a friend who was living in Washington, DC. The friend was attending graduate school at the School of Advanced International Studies (SAIS) at Johns Hopkins University, a top program for international affairs. After learning more about the school and attending a few events with her friend, Angela was impressed with what the school had to offer and decided to apply.

She was accepted. To ease the transition to life as a graduate student, Angela's parents agreed to assist her partially with tuition costs during the first year. To make ends meet, she taught German and French part time and in her second year secured a merit scholarship.

"I was always working," Angela remembers. "I really believe this instilled in me a strong work ethic and discipline — having to be on time and knowing what people expect of you." She recalls how in Germany she tutored less-gifted peers at school and at Bryn Mawr she waitressed in the mornings before classes.

While in graduate school, Angela met and married her first husband, a fellow international affairs student from the Netherlands, who aspired to enter the Dutch Foreign Service. She was young and very much in love; in hindsight, she considers that her youth may have played a role in the eventual end of the marriage.

Upon graduation from SAIS, Angela got a job working for a German news magazine, where she was excited to make a living doing what she loved — writing. Although she was recruited with the promise of receiving formal training, she was disappointed to find that her position was, in fact, no more than a "glorified secretary." She left after less than a year.

Reevaluating her options again, Angela decided to return to her other love — international affairs. During the summer between her first and second years of graduate school, Angela had spent a productive summer working for the World Bank. She decided her best bet was to reapply there for a full-time position. Once in the interview at the World Bank, Angela encountered a blatant display of discrimination regarding her personal life as a married woman. "At that time, things were really different. Employers could even ask for medical records showing if you were on birth control pills to determine whether or not they should bother investing in you." The interviewer told her frankly that they did not want to recruit her into the young professionals program because she was married and her husband, then a PhD student, was not yet settled. Unfortunately, she would find that this would not be the last time that she would have this type of conversation.

Despite the initial setback, Angela persisted and was eventually hired by the World Bank but at a less-prestigious entry level. She stayed there for only a few months. With her husband now about to enter the foreign service, and feeling less than thrilled with her initial reception at the World Bank, Angela agreed to go where her husband's work took them. This was never a problem for her in the beginning of her career. Throughout their travels, Angela was content to work in various jobs and did not give too much consideration to her career path. "At the time, I was just 24 years old. I didn't have the faintest idea what I really wanted to do. I didn't have any real goals." Moreover, her husband's career gave her the opportunity to see many parts of the world — a dream that she had nurtured since childhood and was excited to see fulfilled.

The couple went to live in Paris for one year, where Angela worked as an office manager. Although the culture and lifestyle in Paris were wonderful, balancing work and married life was difficult. As in most places at that time, the French working environment was not hospitable to career women. All the shops were closed in the evenings, meaning there was never time to run errands or get groceries. Only those women who had no day jobs were able to get their shopping done.

When her husband's work took them to the Netherlands, Angela worked at Shell Oil. Then, when his work took them to Bangkok, Thailand, she did not work at all. It was the mid-seventies, and given the country's precarious political situation and social unrest triggered by the dictatorial military regime, Angela was advised against taking a job. Instead, she spent her time exploring the exotic country and the fascinating diversity it had to offer. For someone who had lived only in Western societies, the mix of cultures in Thailand, with its Chinese, Buddhist, and Muslim influences, was truly an eye-opening experience, giving her the rich insight that life can take many different forms and shapes.

Eventually, her husband's work took them back to the US, where he worked at the Netherlands Consulate in New York City. Once in New York, Angela decided to apply for a position at the UN, as her visa status limited her employment options. After all, she had experience working with the World Bank, a high-quality education, and exposure to different cultures. She was also fluent in several languages, including German, French, English, Dutch, and Spanish — that last language she had learned on a whim to communicate better with Spanish-speaking friends in graduate school. It was 1977.

Taking Chances

Within two weeks of her application, Angela was hired as an editor/writer for UN publications—a seemingly perfect fit for someone with a talent for writing and a love of international affairs. With her English degree and international background, Angela fit right in. The job wasn't very glamorous, but she learned a lot and was quickly able to impress many of her colleagues. What Angela learned during this first year would stay with her for decades to come, as it developed within her certain core skills in effective collaboration and management. Within a year of starting the position, Angela was headhunted internally to apply for a position in the Executive Office of the Secretary-General.

"I was recruited at the P-2 entry level. In the personnel interview, the male interviewer said, 'Well, you know, you have a husband and so that means you won't need a salary for this position.' He then tried to imply that my previous work experience was somehow irrelevant to the position and that I may want to consider volunteering with them instead. I was so upset and so disgusted by this argument." She admits that later, at home, she cried about it. Then, after collecting herself, she wrote a letter to the interviewer's supervisor, who was also male. In the letter, Angela did not mention specific remarks of the interviewer; instead, she chose to emphasize the fact that the interviewer failed to see the relevance of her previous work experience when, in reality, she was an exceptionally good fit for the job. Upon receipt of her letter, the supervisor immediately called and offered her the position. The experience taught Angela a crucial lesson about speaking up when she really wanted something. More importantly, as a woman, she felt it was important to refrain from using gender as a reason for complaint. Her qualifications, experience, and determination were all that mattered.

Though in her younger years there were no female role models to emulate, Angela came across one such person early in her career at the UN. "Every year, on March 8, we celebrated International Women's Day at the UN. There were panelists who discussed various issues of interest at the time, including on women. I remember one year when there was a woman at the D-1 (director) level; I thought 'wow.' It was really rare at the time." The memory stands out to Angela as a moment when she received real-life evidence that something like that—achieving a director level—was possible for women, possible for her.

Angela went on to spend four years in the Office of the Secretary-General and later worked with the United Nations Development Programme (UNDP). This time, Angela and her first husband were sent to Jakarta, Indonesia. It was the 1980s. Once in Indonesia, she encountered the same salary issues yet again. She was married, why did she need a salary? It was frustrating.

Angela stayed in Jakarta for three years with the UNDP. In addition to the professional demands of the position, living in Indonesia was also culturally demanding. With a population that was 98 percent Muslim, the pressure to assimilate was very strong at times. "'Why don't you fast with us, Ibu (Ms.) Angela?' they would ask me. It was very important to them that I show solidarity, as they believed it would help us work together better. They wore the same uniforms, fasted together during Ramadan, and pledged allegiance to the flag once a month to celebrate their independence. I would think, 'But that is not my flag; it's not my country; it's not my religion.' But they gently insisted on that show of togetherness. They wanted to know that I was 'one of them' so that we could work together towards a common goal." Angela believes that cultural sensitivity is an important part of any international job and that it pays to be mindful of what your colleagues value the most. The experience taught her the importance of having the grace to accept what you cannot change in support of a greater good; it also taught her the importance of cultivating an appreciation for others' viewpoints—one of the core components of effective management and leadership.

"I've worked in many places during my career at the UN, and people sometimes say that you shouldn't stay in a place too long and run the risk of changing yourself by assimilating too much. But I believe that it really helps to learn the language and the culture of the place where you are living, because it gives you a window into the people. You don't have to negate yourself. You can remain yourself and also learn to appreciate where other people are coming from."

This firm commitment to understanding others played a pivotal role in one of the most exciting and rewarding moments of Angela's UN career so far. In the early 1990s, Angela was part of the team of the Personal Representative of the Secretary-General for the Central American Peace Process to end the civil war in El Salvador. Despite intense negotiations brokered by the secretary-general and his personal representative, progress was slow, because it was difficult to get inputs from the five guerrilla organizations that made up the FMLN. However, it was crucial to integrate their voices into the new political framework to prevent the recurrence of similar precarious situations, especially given that the guerrillas had many sympathizers who were not represented at the negotiating table. The negotiators also had to keep in mind the fact that once heard, demands and concerns of the guerrillas

Inspecting the construction of new UN office buildings
in Nairobi, 2009

had to be taken seriously, if not entirely accommodated.

"Many of the guerrillas were fighters who had never had proper, formal education. We had to make conscientious efforts not to overlook their arguments based on their lack of education." To add another layer of complexity, civilian police forces in the country were not used to working with women, and Angela had to go the extra mile to make herself heard.

Despite these differences, difficulties, and challenges, the process was largely a successful one. This is what Angela loves most about the experience: "We were faced with seemingly intractable problems between the government and the guerrillas. But we succeeded. It shows you that even in the face of big hurdles, with focus and hard work, you *can* jump over them. Working on negotiations on a topic as huge as peace and security is not a typical office job. In the field, there's an immediate reward to what you are doing and a satisfaction to being able to move things."

In 1995, following the excitement of her work in El Salvador and a subsequent assignment in the Office of the Secretary-General as a political director, Angela decided to take a managerial position at UN headquarters. Many of her friends and colleagues were somewhat skeptical. How could she possibly take a managerial position after her work in the field in countries as diverse as Indonesia and El Salvador? However, Angela now had a clear vision in mind for her career. In the new managerial position that she was taking on, Angela would be responsible for a budget of US $50 million and oversee 250 people. "There's no way to substitute for that kind of responsibility," Angela remarks. She knew that in order to fulfill her dream, she needed to have solid experience managing budgets and people. She believes that the experience she acquired and the level of responsibility she handled then provided a fertile groundwork for where she is today.

Looking Forward and Lessons Learned

Throughout her career, Angela managed to maintain a strong sense of the family ideal that had been instilled in her from childhood, an ideal of a happy, married life raising children. After all, this was the model on which her childhood was based. However, unlike her mother, who played the role of wife and stay-at-home mother, Angela played the role of career woman. Angela and her first husband met when she was just 21. By today's standards, she married very young. For instance, as of 2008, the average age for a first marriage for a woman in Germany was 30.[4] Angela had remained strongly committed to the marriage even as she and her husband pursued their careers. However, there came a point in her late thirties when she knew that it simply was not working—a very difficult reality to accept. "It was very devastating at the time. I felt like I was a failure." Throughout the divorce proceedings, Angela did very well professionally, continuing to be recognized and rising within the UN. Although she was able to maintain her sense of professionalism, it was difficult not to become distracted.

"As an employer, it makes me more considerate of what people are going through. Personal circumstances can make people unstable for a bit. I'm lucky that I came out of it okay."

Angela has been married to her second husband for nearly 20 years now. "It was difficult to be back on the dating scene," she laughs. Unsure of where to begin, and preoccupied with her work and various social activities, Angela stayed on the periphery of dating activities until a close family friend invited her to a dinner party and said to her, "I know someone you'd really hit it off with." Smiling, Angela says, "Well, my second husband was there...and honestly, there was no looking back." The years since then proved that the friend was right. Her husband, an entrepreneur with a technology and banking background, has been very supportive of Angela's working life. "He understands that my career is important to me and that it involves some personal sacrifices. Domestic duties often get short shrift, and there are frequent absences due to travel." For instance: "When the offer was made to join a peacekeeping mission in Africa, he was fully in sync with my decision to go," she says. And, to her delight, he was eager to share that part of her life, visiting whenever possible. Before departure, her husband presented her with a digital camera so that pictures could be exchanged immediately over the Internet. "That was so incredibly helpful in keeping in touch," Angela laughs. "I sent pictures of my daily life in the mission, and he supplied pictures of dinners with friends and how my plants were doing in the apartment at home!"

When asked if there is anything that she would have done differently, Angela smiles. "I don't think so...there was no well-trodden path to follow. I came of age in the bra-burning era and that kind of strident feminism was not for me. There had to be other ways." Angela admits that she was very lucky to have parents who strongly supported her education and encouraged her to broaden her horizon beyond the small town of Hameln or even of Germany. "They never doubted my ability to succeed, and having this trust and confidence is absolutely crucial."

Angela confesses that she did not foresee a set career path until maybe her late thirties; it was only then that she began to think about it more seriously. Upon reflection, she says, "I think it's good to have goalposts in mind for your career, but that wasn't me at 20 or even 30. I think the most important thing is to be open to opportunities and to pursue them consistently and with passion. Don't be afraid to try new things and take a new path. I sometimes moved laterally rather than trying to move only to the next rung up." Angela's driving motivation throughout her career was always to do something she was passionate about. She did not just want to be the next rung in the ladder; she wanted to enjoy her path and fill each step with something exciting, stimulating, and meaningful. Moreover, she wanted to do it on her terms, whether as a woman or a German or anything else.

Regardless of what one's path may be, Angela firmly believes one must speak up about what he or she really wants. "You will have no chance of getting what you want or to where you want to go, unless you speak up," she says. With this frame of mind, she succeeded in having "a long and distinguished career in the UN,"[5] having served on key posts, including the Assistant Secretary-General for Political Affairs, Deputy Special Representative of the Secretary-General in a peacekeeping mission in Africa, Assistant Secretary-General for General Assembly and Conference Management, and Director in the Department of Public Information.

When Angela was rising through the ranks of the UN, sometimes as the first woman to hold a given post, some people questioned her ability to deliver on a mandate. They would invariably ask, "How can you do it? You are the first woman to have this job." Angela did not let such questions undermine her confidence. She maintained the logic, "If you have a job, you have to fill it."

Therefore, what does it take to be a woman leader? Angela explains that there are some differences between male and female

With Secretary-General Ban Ki-moon, 2010

leadership. "I'm speaking generally, but oftentimes, you'll find that men will state their views very decidedly, whereas women are a lot more willing to entertain other sides of the argument." She has also found that there tends to be more conciliatory and inclusive approaches to women leadership. On the flipside, that willingness to listen to other points of view can result in problems for women managers. "I find that many women are not good at saying 'no,' myself included. We try to be accommodating." Angela also finds that many stereotypes about women still plague them in senior leadership positions. "There tends to be an assumption that women in higher positions don't get along — kind of a Queen Bee syndrome. But actually, I find this quality, this competitiveness, occurring in both genders." Angela notes that the antidote to dealing with stereotypes against women is to be totally professional, factual, and unemotional when it comes to work.

For any leader, male or female, Angela believes that humility is perhaps the greatest quality. "Leaders should not have a big head or believe that they are above those that they are leading." When she made it to the director level (D-2), managing some 250 staff and reporting directly to the assistant secretary-general, her husband reminded her that she now had "corruptible" power. It is easy for one to feel important when occupying high positions, but they have to remember that they were once *not* important. "Use your power wisely. It is easy to abuse power, so we must always be reflective about what we are doing. No one is infallible." Moreover, Angela believes that "occasional career setbacks are beneficial in providing a sense of perspective and reality and that helps when one gets to the top. Being passed over for another job or for a promotion is difficult to accept at the time," she explains, "but it also makes you realize that you cannot always be successful and must soldier on with good grace."

Another critical leadership quality is listening and admitting that some opinions are better than one's own. In order to do so, a leader should be accessible to staff and shed the "I am the boss, so I decide" mentality. It is important to accept diverse opinions and build a team spirit. However, a leader should never forget that one is a leader; they must believe in their own capabilities enough to say, when necessary, *no*. When Angela was a mid-level manager, she had an assistant with strong opinions. While respecting the assistant's opinions, Angela had to put her foot down and implement her own decisions to avoid consumptive delays. Doing so takes confidence in oneself as an expert and a decision-maker.

Also important to a leader is vision. The vision that Angela refers to is not a roadmap to achieving some agreed goals, but a sense of purpose and common understanding. A leader should be able to motivate his or her staff to accomplish something collectively, not drag them into a project that they are not eager to partake. Creating a vision and getting staff buy-in entails a series of steps. The first step is talking to them through group meetings and, for some recalcitrant ones, one-on-one meetings. Angela emphasizes that a leader should clearly communicate what he or she wants to achieve and try to get staff excited about the idea, especially in public service organizations where there can be high levels of institutional resistance. Unless people are truly committed to a new idea, they will act at best slowly and, where feasible, try to sabotage its implementation. Hence, a leader must communicate clearly and consistently what needs to be done and how it is beneficial for everyone involved.

Furthermore, good leadership is built on integrity. Setting an example and making people follow their own volition is one of the most potent tools of leadership. According to Angela, a leader can fundamentally change the way people work in the present and influence their work ethics and behavior in the future. Angela recalls an experience where her boss blatantly lied to her about why she was passed over for promotion. It was a job that was supposed to be awarded on merit, but was given to someone else for political reasons. The moment she discovered the lie, Angela promised that she would never risk her honor and respect by telling lies, even "white" ones.

"These types of experiences, though tough and stressful, give you a sense of humility. They bring you back to reality." She extracted another lesson: that the selection process can be an agonizing experience for hopeful applicants, and that they deserve to be told the truth. Angela therefore gets in touch with interviewed applicants directly and explains her selection decision to them individually. Although time-consuming, such a practice adds transparency to the process and prevents potential antagonism that can rise from the murkiness of UN politics.

Finally, Angela believes that it is incumbent upon a leader to recognize staff contributions and sustain their interest in performing a given job. At the time when she was appointed Under-Secretary-General for Management, there were reports of palpable tension and low morale among many staff in the organization due to the perception that the management "did not know the staff and did not feel a personal link with most of them," giving them an impression that "figures matter more than people."[6] Angela was determined to reverse such a negative and demoralizing atmosphere by exercising "good" leadership.

As the head of management, Angela realizes that many of her staff are responsible for unglamorous jobs—grounds keeping and building maintenance, for example. In this context, staff in the Department of Management can fall prey to feelings of being outside the center of activity and even boredom and anonymity. One of the initiatives that she has taken to tackle this problem was to utilize the information portal designed exclusively for UN staff, called i-seek. This website, which is available only within the UN system, contains stories on the latest developments of the organization and provides a central point where all the UN offices around the world can get together online and keep each other informed. Angela took advantage of this platform and, through articles, recognized the contributions of general staff whose services often go unnoticed. She also created a suggestion box on i-seek, soliciting comments from staff about changes they want to see in management. Her team meticulously goes through each suggestion and gets back to the individuals with follow-up measures. This spirit of openness and recognition in the quest to change things for the better is one of the characteristic aspects of Angela's leadership and management style.

Regarding how she handles criticism, Angela admits, "Nobody likes to be criticized. But it comes with the job and we try to cope with it." Instead of taking offense at criticism, Angela tries to analyze what is behind it and sometimes resorts to humor— even self-deprecating humor—to help relieve the tension that affects everyone involved. And such graciousness should be complemented by assertiveness. Women, especially, need to be able to assert themselves to be heard and not dismissed.

Oftentimes, the UN's multicultural environment provides ample opportunity for criticism and misunderstandings, because what is appropriate in certain cultures can be interpreted as incompetence or disrespect in other cultures. For instance, current

Secretary-General Ban Ki-moon has been criticized for practicing "quiet diplomacy," which is interpreted in certain quarters as weak leadership and lack of charisma. However, as underscored by the secretary-general himself and a host of commentators, particularly from the Asian region, soft-spokenness and humility are considered characters of virtuous and effective leadership. Angela agrees and supports Mr. Ban's assessment that "while the United Nations is an inter-governmental body, you come with different background, you come with all different leadership style, you come with all different resources. Therefore, we need to be harmonious and we have to be able to respect the culture, tradition, and leadership style of each and every leader. This is very important."[7]

Finally, the ability to be truly comfortable in one's own womanhood, while still embodying those characteristics necessary for success, is a lesson that all women in the professional world must learn. Having grown up in a culture where assertiveness in women was not prized, Angela found it difficult early on in her career to assert her opinions and stand her ground. "I was instilled with a very stereotypical image of how women should be through the culture I grew up in and through my own family experience. Yet, that's not at all what I am like now. You are imprinted by culture early on and then when things are different, it can be a bit of a shock." Dealing with this shock requires the ability to adapt. Interestingly, one tends to find that if she can successfully adapt and grow to meet new demands and challenges, so too will the world around her begin to change, expanding to include new conceptions of what it is to be a woman.

Angela advises young women today to "find a job that motivates you, where you can learn, and look for change when it becomes routine and boring. Don't only think of moving up; expose yourself to new experiences, tackle new challenges, stretch yourself, learn another language. And if you get to a powerful position, fill it with grace and humility: don't ever forget many others are less fortunate."

Being a Woman

Angela reminds us that times have really changed for aspiring young women. She came of age when the pool of willing and qualified women for public service was relatively small and gender biases were very strong. Still, the challenges she faces as a woman in power today continue to be challenges that all women must face in some way or another as a result of how society attempts to define them and their place in the world. Angela's response to these societal attempts was, and has always been, to define her own world.

Susana Malcorra

New York, 2009 / UN Photo, Eskinder Debebe

Susana Malcorra

On March 14, 2008, Secretary-General Ban Ki-moon appointed Ms. Susana Malcorra as Under-Secretary-General and Head of the Department of Field Support.

The Head of the Department of Field Support leads staff across 32 field operations, comprised of over 100,000 military, police, and civilian personnel. The department supports and makes budgetary, tactical, and human resource decisions related to peacekeeping, humanitarian, and political field operations throughout the globe.

"Please, follow me, welcome," Susana Malcorra says briskly with a hearty handshake as she leads us from the waiting area to her office. Though small in stature in a smartly cut tan suit, when you first meet her, Susana Malcorra's presence easily fills the entire room.

According to Susana, the position she holds is a "very interesting, albeit demanding" job. There is always something happening and, as a result, one ends up being a "firefighter" most of the time. In addition to figuring out logistics and resource requirements for the various operations happening throughout the globe, there are also sensitivities to consider, both political and cultural, depending on the situation at hand. "In order to do this job you MUST be passionate about it. You must sometimes be willing to subtract yourself from the equation in order to get things done..."

Born to Excel

"I was an only child — and I believe this is something that is very important to who I am today." Susana grew up in what she calls a "working class" urban neighborhood in Rosario, Argentina, the country's third-largest city behind Buenos Aires and Cordoba, with just under one million inhabitants. It is located on the west bank of the Paraná River in the east-central part of the country, where it has historically served as a river port.[1]

With more than 92 percent of the population living in metropolitan areas, Argentina is a highly urbanized country as well as a member of the G-20 economies, a group of 19 industrialized countries and the European Union, which acts as a cooperative and consultative body on matters related to the international financial system. However, despite the natural resources and industrial wealth of the country, Argentina has faced economic crises throughout much of the twentieth century, and it is home to the type of income inequality that characterizes many major South American countries.[2]

Susana describes her family's financial situation when she was growing up as "lower-middle class" and counts her parents as being very hardworking people. Her mother was a housekeeper and her father worked as a laborer throughout her childhood. It was important to both of her parents that Susana grow up to become a professional woman and lead a very good life, as they wanted her to have all of the material comforts that they did not have.

An only child, her family's expectations for Susana were high. Her parents wanted and expected her to have a family, as this was very important culturally, and they also wanted her to be successful professionally. With these expectations firmly in place, Susana did not have much choice but to excel — in everything. From an early age, Susana's parents enrolled her in English and French classes, as well as various music lessons. She was always doing something to further enrich her education and expose her to new things; her parents hoped that these advantages would help Susana figure out what her path should be and ensure that she would be successful once she started down on it.

"I think that the expectations they placed on me, their only child, developed in me the basic value and understanding that I had to work hard. I look at my son now—he's in his twenties—and he gets so much enjoyment out of slowly discovering his path and his career. Back then, it was different—you did what you had to do."

Overall, Susana had a very happy childhood. She went to a good all-girls Catholic school, did very well academically, and had good friends. Though she appreciated the neighborhood she grew up in, it was clear that Susana's path would be different from her peers. "The expectation for most girls in my neighborhood was that they would graduate from high school and immediately get married and have children. My parents expected different things from me and I expected different things from myself."

Culturally, Catholicism is an important part of Argentine society and serves as the country's unofficial religion; until 1994, the country's president and vice president both had to be Roman Catholic.[3] This cultural context provided the foundation for the type of family life that was expected of Susana and her classmates and served as a bond with the society she grew up in. Experiencing a religious culture outside of her own would serve as an important and eye-opening experience for Susana.

At the age of 16, on her own initiative, Susana did a one-year exchange program in the US. She was placed in a small town in Missouri, where most of the neighborhood was Protestant. "My host family was Protestant and I went to church with them. This was very different for me because back home, EVERYone was Catholic! The whole experience really opened up my eyes to a different way of life for the first time. It showed me firsthand that it's a really big world."

Susana emphasizes that her exchange experience was a "big deal" at the time because the world was not as global then as it is now. It was very significant and progressive of her parents to be supportive of Susana doing the exchange program. Always strong proponents of her growth and development, Susana's parents understood how important it was to allow her to go abroad, even though it was a sacrifice on their part.

Susana's exposure to and interest in so many things made it unclear exactly what she should do after high school. Although she excelled at and was engaged in all of her subjects, she had a keen interest in the sciences. It was especially rare for women to be interested in the sciences at the time, though that small fact did not diminish her interest. "I didn't really know exactly what I wanted to be for sure when I was growing up. At first, I thought about maybe becoming a lawyer or a biochemist," she laughs. "Then, when I was on exchange in the US, I became interested in becoming a nuclear engineer after learning more about nuclear energy."

After some deliberation about the various types of engineering, Susana decided that after graduation she would pursue electrical engineering at the University of Rosario, which happened to be the one school in Argentina that offered her intended field of study. Once enrolled at the university, Susana immediately became aware of just how exceptional her choice was. "I was the ONLY woman in my entire class. It was quite a different experience from what I was used to back in my old neighborhood. I went from attending an all-girls Catholic high school to being the only girl in the entire class."

Although it was very different for her, Susana did not have much trouble adjusting. Whenever any of the guys in her classes gave her trouble because of her gender, she simply told herself it was their problem, not hers. Instead of letting her minority status get the best of her, she learned quickly to make herself a part of whatever team she found herself in and did not allow herself to feel like she was an outsider.

"They got used to me," she remarks simply. "They would tease me, call me 'Pedro' because I was like one of the guys, but I did not take offense to it. In fact, I took it as a compliment. It means that they considered me their equal. That's the attitude I had to adopt in order to stay focused."

Woman Engineer, Woman Pioneer

Like most of the women we have profiled, Susana confesses that she did not really have a set plan at the start of her career. In fact, she believes that this is a good thing—not to always plan everything. "You must learn to surf on the waves of opportunities," she says, a rather poetic way of describing how to be open to and navigate through the various possibilities that life has to offer.

Of course, sometimes life presents us with things that we would rather not accept or deal with, both professionally and personally. During her first year away at college, Susana's father passed away suddenly, leaving her mother without financial support at home in her old neighborhood. To support herself and her mother, Susana took on various jobs while at school, teaching math, working as a teaching assistant, and in a lab. Family was and still is extremely important to Susana, and she took on the responsibility of supporting her mother without question or hesitation.

Susana worked hard both in and outside of her classes; as the only woman in her graduating class, Susana ended her experience at the University of Rosario with the highest respect and admiration of her classmates and professors. Towards the end of her studies, one of Susana's professors, who happened to be the chief of a major multinational company, approached Susana about her plans after graduation. Through his professional connections, he had gotten wind of an exciting opportunity with a major European company and wanted to recommend Susana for a job. Susana gladly took him up on his offer.

Susana went through eight rounds of interviews that culminated in a final meeting with the company's director of personnel. As she had hoped, the director informed Susana that she had passed all of the previous interviews with flying colors. Unfortunately for her, they could not give her the position. He told her plainly to her face that it was because she was a woman. The year was 1978.

Susana remembers it clearly. "It really hurt. It upset me so much. At that point, I thought to myself, 'Why didn't they just throw my application out when they received my resume and saw my name?' They knew I was a woman then. But I believe that they were hoping to find some reason not to hire me by having me go through the eight rounds of interviews. When they couldn't find any other reasons, they just had to finally tell me the truth. 'No, it's because you're a woman.'"

The experience was especially difficult for Susana because it was the first time she had been truly made to feel like an outsider. Prior to that devastating experience, she had been accepted in all-male environments or, at the very least, had always found a way to make them accept her. She says now, "I'm happy they didn't hire me, but at the time, it was difficult."

Somewhat serendipitously, that same day, Susana saw an advertisement for a position with IBM Argentina. In the ad, it said that they were looking for both male and female engineers. Susana picked herself back up and sent in her application. "I thought—great! Now I have a real chance. Then, when I got into the interview, to test me, the interviewer said, 'Well, I don't know if you can handle the position, you're a woman...'" With her previous interview experience still a fresh wound, Susana did not hesitate to give the interviewer a piece of her mind. "I got so angry at him!" she laughs. "I really told him something. I left the interview convinced that they would never call me, but then a few weeks later, I had the job!"

Susana stayed at IBM for 15 years. She recalls her time with IBM as a truly great, challenging, and rewarding experience, one that provided her with the opportunity to go to the US for a rotational training program in which she received the chance to learn directly from company leadership.

Towards the end of her career at IBM, Susana found out about a number of promising positions at Telecom Argentina, the major phone company for all of northern Argentina, including the entire city of Buenos Aires. The company was looking for managers to help them meet new business demands. It was the early 1990s and privatization reforms were sweeping across the country. In order to put the country on the path toward economic liberalization, whole sectors had been deregulated and businesses were shifting from government ownership to privatization.[4]

All of these changes required new skills from business people who had formerly been working under the very different regulations and demands of state-owned enterprises. Susana was excited to have the opportunity to take on the challenge of helping the company adapt to these new demands. She applied to an opening and was quickly accepted for a management position.

Once at Telecom Argentina, Susana hit the ground running. "I started off managing 5,000 people. I developed major changes in the makeup of the business portfolio and I began implementing necessary human resource changes." At that time, many people in the company had come from the public sector (as the country was just beginning to privatize many industries) and there was a great need for people with new private sector skills. Susana and her colleagues had to come up with different standards for hiring and for performance measurement.

As this was a time of tremendous change for the company and for the country as a whole, Susana had to quickly acquire the leadership skills necessary to manage the diverse interests of various stakeholders, including internal staff, union groups, and regulatory bodies. "It was a very difficult time and a very interesting time," she remembers. Despite the many challenging situations she faced, Susana's hard work eventually paid off; she ended up becoming Telecom Argentina's first female CEO.

Susana reflects on her experience at Telecom Argentina by comparing it to her first job with IBM. "Although there were a lot of difficult moments at IBM, it was primarily a sales-driven career; the difficulty was all about competing at an individual level to achieve sales targets. It was a very high-risk, high-reward environment. Telecom Argentina, on the other hand, was difficult in a different way. It was all about managing the various moving parts to stay competitive in our industry and to achieve targets on a group level."

Competing on a group level can prove to be very difficult in the best of times, as it is complicated to align the often-diverging interests of various stakeholders towards meeting common goals. When tasked with managing those same stakeholders in a time of tremendous change and in the face of uncontrollable external circumstances, Susana discovered that it could prove to be virtually impossible.

Throughout the mid 1990s, a number of external economic shocks and fundamental systemic failures resulted in a marked economic decline throughout much of South America. In 2001, the full brunt of the financial crisis hit the country and Telecom Argentina was not spared. Susana and her colleagues did their best to weather the storm, but in the end, it was simply not enough. "Eventually, we had to file for Chapter 11 bankruptcy.[i] And I was the CEO; I was the one who had to announce the news to everyone in the company." Because Telecom Argentina was a publicly owned company, Susana was also required to go to Wall Street and announce the unfortunate situation to the company's shareholders. She considers this moment to be the most difficult moment of her career.

"I ended up leaving Telecom Argentina soon after we declared

---

i. Chapter 11 is a form of bankruptcy that requires a fundamental restructuring of a company's assets and debts. It is generally the most expensive form of bankruptcy and is usually considered as a last resort after all other options have been considered. Source: Investopedia.com.

Addressing the Security Council on United Nations peacekeeping operations, New York, January 2009 / UN Photo, Jenny Rockett

bankruptcy. The board felt that they needed someone who understood debt management, as that would be very important for Telecom Argentina going forward, and I simply didn't have any experience with that." In addition, after the tremendous stress of the past several years, Susana also felt it was time to move on. "It's very difficult to build something and then to see it all fall apart," she says. "It was very hard."

Turning Challenge into Opportunity

Shaken by her experiences with Telecom Argentina, Susana decided to take a step back and seriously think about what she wanted to do next in her career. She did some soul searching and felt that one of her unfulfilled passions was to make a difference in the international public arena. Susana's willingness to remain open to new opportunities facilitated her ability to bounce back in an unexpected way after a crushing defeat. It was 2002.

"I told headhunters that I wanted to do something totally

different from what I had done before. I told them that they could now consider me for positions in nongovernmental and multilateral organizations. I had a new interest in the international public sector."

While she waited for the recruiters to come through, she did consulting work to keep busy. Then in 2003, Susana got a call from a recruiter saying that the UN World Food Programme (WFP) in Rome wanted to find an exceptional Latin American woman to run the organization. "At the time, I had no clue what the WFP was! But the more I learned about it, the more I found it was really right for me."

The WFP is the world's largest humanitarian agency tasked with the mission of fighting hunger worldwide. In emergencies, the WFP provides food to those who need it, whether they are victims of war or civil conflict or natural disasters. The job would require acute operational abilities and the integrity to make tough and strategic decisions, in addition to a compassionate and service-oriented perspective.

Susana discussed the issue with her husband, a civil engineer whom she met at university through their shared interest in politics. "We always consult with each other for every major decision and decide what the best investment is for the both of us, for our shared future, and for our son." As Susana's husband learned more about the WFP and the scope of its work, he confirmed Susana's own feeling when he said simply to her, "that's you." Susana and her family picked up and moved to Rome. She started her position in July 2004.

Susana was a natural in her new position with the WFP and quickly gained the respect and admiration of her colleagues. After a couple of years enjoying her new life in Rome, Susana received a recommendation to apply for an under-secretary-general position at the UN in New York. After considering the opportunity with her husband, the couple decided that they were very happy in Rome and so Susana politely declined. Despite her initial declination, Susana was invited to interview for the position before a panel in

Memorial service for the United Nations staff victims of the Haiti earthquake, New York, March 2010 / UN Photo, Paulo Filgueiras

New York along with several other candidates. Intrigued, Susana reconsidered the prospect and decided to accept the invitation to interview.

Round after round, she succeeded, and she eventually found herself interviewing with the secretary-general. The interview was a success. With her achievements as director of the World Food Programme and with vast operational experience in the private sector under her belt, Susana was a perfect fit. She was appointed as Under-Secretary-General of Field Operations in 2008.

The many unexpected twists and turns that she took on the path to her career at the UN have given Susana a unique and inspiring perspective on her career and on life in general. "We can only make plans based on our own limited understanding of the world and its possibilities. Therefore, it's important to be open to new opportunities and the future that those opportunities might open up for us." Susana believes that the young women just starting out in their careers should know that there is a world of opportunity and it is hard to see it clearly from where they are today. "Follow your heart and trust yourself. If in the end it doesn't work out the way you thought it would, there will be other opportunities to pursue."

Susana and her husband have developed an excellent career partnership in this regard, as they always try to make choices that are the best investment for both of them based on the information that they have available. Rather than have one career dominate the other, they work together to see the value in various possibilities. "Once when I was at IBM, I was asked to work in the US for one year as a part of the manager development program. As it was a major opportunity for me and would ultimately benefit both of us, my husband agreed to move to the US for my work. He arranged a leave of absence from his job and did an MBA course, which also furthered his career and, in turn, benefitted both of us."

Juggling Family and Work

As her career advanced, Susana found that balancing work and family—as is the case for all working wives and mothers—can be difficult. "I have a very supportive partner," she says. "We both have independent careers. For instance, right now I am in New York City for my work and he is in Madrid for his work." Susana believes that she is very lucky to have such an independent, yet supportive, partnership.

The couple also worked successfully together in raising their bright and talented son. Susana describes how it was important to them to provide a stable home support system for their son, given that they were both busy professionals. "The way we handled it was partly cultural. When my son was young, my mom lived in an apartment next door to us and the help we had around the house was like our family."

Of course, it wasn't always perfect. Susana recalls a time when she felt that she had dropped the ball in providing the supportive environment that her son needed. Her son, then 13, was taking

French at school and had asked Susana, who is fluent in French, to help him prepare for his exam. On that particular day, Susana was held up at the office and ended up arriving home much later than expected, missing the time to help him study. "He was so upset with me that it made me consider quitting working. But, when I said that to him, he looked at me as if he couldn't believe what he had heard. He said to me, 'Mom, I only wanted you to be here when I asked you to; I don't want you to quit your work. If you were here all day, you would drive us all nuts!'"

With a supportive family and a high-profile career, it seems that Susana has managed to "have it all." Susana is deeply appreciative of all of the wonderful things in her life and finds that having such a full life sometimes leaves little time for the things that one loves to do. "The one thing I don't have time for is myself. At the end of the day, when you are a busy person, you end up being the one to spare when it comes to what needs to get done. I love to read, but I simply don't have the time for it. When it comes down to it, I end up being the variable part of the equation."

Though her current position keeps her busy, she believes it is very worthwhile. That said, due to the nature of the work, it is not without its difficult moments. "I would have to say the most difficult moment for me was dealing with the 2010 earthquake in Haiti. I was in charge of supporting the mission to help the victims. We had lost many important members of our leadership there. It was difficult balancing the operational logistics, the personal cases, and the family situations, while trying to remain professional and avoid becoming emotional. We had to deliver despite the circumstances."

Through that experience, Susana learned how far it is possible to push oneself in order to get things done. Although the gap between reality and what needs to happen can sometimes be quite large, it's important to keep working at it to the best of your ability. Filling that gap properly, however, can be quite difficult, as the parameters and the targets in a humanitarian crisis are not as

Department of Peacekeeping Operations Heads of Military Components Conference, August 2010 / UN Photo, Paulo Filgueiras

clear and concrete as in the private sector.

Susana explains this difficulty further by discussing the differences between the private sector and her work at the UN. When Susana worked at the WFP, it was similar to the private sector in that it's primarily an operationally focused mission. Now, as head of field operations, she must manage on a diplomatic level within the politics of the UN system, while also informing the decision-making process with down-to-earth, concrete goals.

"The private sector is very results-oriented. Success is measured in dollars, your financial statements, your return on investment. It's easier to align people with these kinds of concrete goals. At the end of the day, a decision is made and you simply move forward. At the UN, however, the objectives are often very unclear. Defining success at the UN can be as intangible as defining success in motherhood — how exactly do you measure that? It's qualitative. At the UN, you must move forward based on consensus and this consensus must be achieved in a multicultural environment where there is a very different understanding of the issues across cultures. You have to bring these two sides (the concrete and the intangible) of the equation together in order to be successful. It's a huge challenge."

Despite the complexities of working within uncertain situations, Susana believes that every day at the UN is exciting and valuable. The most exciting part for her is being in the field because that is where you can see tangible impact. "Like most large organizations, the UN has many problems, but it is also amazing. At the UN, we are there to serve people who need us. It's amazing to see how we can transform things. It's incredibly inspiring. It recharges my batteries."

Looking Forward and Lessons Learned

Looking back on her career, Susana says that there is not anything that she would have done differently — she is pretty happy with her life as it is. "I'm sure there are things that I could have done differently, but it's always easy to make decisions with the next day's paper," she smiles. "It's always going to be imperfect. But, I think that if it all nets positive, then I'm comfortable with that."

Equally important to "netting positive," says Susana, is to trust your instincts when choosing your career path. "You can be a risk taker, but you also have to ask yourself, is it a reasonable risk? Is it worth it? I've found that the more dedicated I am to a job, and the more responsible and involved I become, the more energy I have. Unless you feel excited about something, you shouldn't do it. If you have doubts about it, don't do it."

Success to Susana is about being happy with what you are doing. "Most of my life I have felt successful, sometimes I have been miserable (and I was in the same position career-wise). Success is definitely about how you feel."

"If people remember you and your contributions, not in the interest of yourself, but in the interest of your organization, to serve others, trying to improve the overall, and you yourself are happy with your contributions, then that is great success...I think that's what I want people to remember me for...continuous improvements."

Susana doesn't believe that there is a single recipe for being a good leader. But one thing Susana does count as a requirement for being a good leader is being a "people person." Essentially, one must have the capacity to empathize and connect with others. "Every culture does this differently," Susana notes. "Ultimately, you must have a sense of vision and a way of bringing people together to achieve that vision. You must have an aspiration or objective for people to organize around, otherwise, they won't be inspired to work together." Once a leader has managed to organize people around an objective, they should also know how to manage those people in the most efficient way to get the job done. "You can't just be a leader and 'walk on water;' you have to also be able to connect to reality and know what the limitations and requirements are for reaching your goals."

Susana admits that like most people who find themselves in positions of power, she does not always do well in all areas of being a great leader. "I think any leader has to be honest and true to themselves and understand the importance of making the best use of their personal strengths, and, sometimes, accepting their personal weaknesses." Susana is very aware that she is better at some aspects of leadership than others. She considers herself very self-critical. "I always push myself. I think this comes from my upbringing with my parents. That feeling that you must excel."

As for criticism from others, Susana believes that she accepts it well. "I am open to constructive criticism. That makes being at the UN difficult — everyone is so polite!" She laughs. "I am very direct and I have no problem with criticism. I'd much rather receive direct criticism (even if it is difficult to hear) so that I can correct the problem."

Although Susana sometimes misses the frankness of the private sector, she values the UN for the respect and dignity that it provides. Susana feels fortunate to have the opportunity to be in a position where she feels that she is pretty close to where a lot of the big discussions about global issues are taking place; she dreams of a world where people of different backgrounds and points of view can talk to each other in a more civil and meaningful way.

"The world has become more extreme in its views and that needs to change. It's time to be balanced and respectful. That is why I value the UN so much. It's the one place where everyone has space to talk. Sure, it doesn't always happen perfectly, but it provides that space."

Finding Your Path

Susana shows us that there are countless ways to define and achieve success; oftentimes, we can find success in ways that we may never have considered before. Susana started as an engineer in the private sector and eventually became the first female CEO of a major telecom company. Faced with defeat, she got back up and reinvented herself in the international public arena. Now, she is making use of her skills and her sense of compassion in a way she never imagined she would.

Rachel Mayanja

New York, 2004

Finding Balance

Rachel Mayanja

On August 12, 2004, then Secretary-General Kofi Annan announced the appointment of Ms. Rachel Mayanja as his Special Adviser on Gender Issues and Advancement of Women. As an assistant under-secretary-general, the Special Adviser on Gender Issues and Advancement of Women is tasked with the mission of promoting and strengthening the implementation of internationally agreed goals on the status of women, including the 2000 Millennium Declaration and the 1995 Beijing Declaration and the Platform for Action.[i] The special adviser also serves as an independent voice and source of knowledge and support on issues that affect women and girls throughout the globe.

One of the first things that catches one's eye upon entering Ms. Mayanja's spacious office on the twelfth floor of a UN building is an assortment of dolls that stand demurely on top of a low cabinet along one side of her office. As her title suggests, Ms. Mayanja is passionately dedicated to women's empowerment, and her dolls, collected from around the world, remind her daily of the countless girls and women

---

i. Adopted by the UN General Assembly in 2000, the Millennium Declaration contains world leaders' resolve "to promote gender equality and the empowerment of women as effective ways to combat poverty, hunger, and disease and to stimulate development that is truly sustainable." The Beijing Declaration and the Platform for Action were adopted at the Fourth World Conference on Women in September 1995 in China to promote and accelerate progress toward gender equality and women's empowerment.

who need help from outside due to poverty, violence, human
trafficking, or any form of oppression. Looking beyond the
colorful traditional dresses that don these dolls and the
beauty of cultural diversity that they represent, Ms. Mayanja
starts her day with the humbling recognition that she carries
the voices of silent girls and women in the international
policymaking arena.

Childhood in Uganda

"Well, there was always someone to play with... and to fight with,"
she says fondly of her large family, a broad smile spreading across
her face. Born in Uganda, Rachel Mayanja was the second oldest
of nine children. As the first-born daughter, she was expected to
take on a leadership role in the family from an early age, helping
with household chores and tending to the care and upbringing
of the younger children. Back then, as is still the case in many
developing countries around the world, girls were expected to do
"certain things" in the household, such as subsistence cultivation,
cooking, and doing laundry for the family. Although there was
often much work to do, Rachel had a "fun childhood," with plenty
of opportunities to get into harmless mischief with her siblings.

Rachel's family belonged to the Kingdom of Buganda, the
largest traditional kingdom in Uganda, which comprises most
of the country's central region, including the Ugandan capital
Kampala. The 5.5 million people of Buganda, known as the Baganda,
currently make up the largest ethnic group in Uganda, representing
approximately 18 percent of the population.[1] Rachel's father was
one of the chiefs in Buganda and was "extremely supportive" of
his daughters. Contrary to Uganda's prevailing cultural norm at
the time, in which women were taught to "accede to the wishes"
of men and—in rural Buganda—even expected to kneel down
when speaking to a man,[2] Rachel's father believed in equal
treatment of boys and girls. Rachel recalls, "From the beginning,

he convinced me that the sky was the limit, and if I wanted, with hard work, I could achieve anything and everything."[3] Such encouragement made Rachel feel "good about being a girl,"[4] a rightful privilege that she wants to extend to other girls around the world.

When Rachel reached primary school age, her father enrolled her in an all-girls boarding school run by British missionaries. The school was one of the best in Uganda, with students consisting primarily of the daughters of the ruling class. When establishing the school, the British missionaries consulted and negotiated with the King of Buganda to determine how students would be selected to attend the school, as well as exactly what they would be taught once enrolled. In addition to receiving a high-quality education, it was also important that the girls receive social and cultural training that would allow them to meet societal expectations. The girls had to be raised "properly," and it was incumbent upon the school to teach them the skills to succeed as wives and mothers—skills they would normally learn had they grown up in their own families surrounded by other female figures. As a result, in addition to traditional subjects like math and science, the school trained the girls in a range of subjects related to housework and childcare.

Throughout primary and secondary school, Rachel was a bright student and excelled in all of her subjects, receiving top scores in math, science, and language arts. Ever since childhood, Rachel had wanted to become a doctor, as she had a deep desire to help people. Unfortunately, being an all-rounded top performer did not guarantee that she would be able to pursue the path she desired upon graduation. "As there was only a certain number of slots for girls to go into medicine or law or teaching, the girls that had scored well in science, but poorly in language arts, were directed towards medicine," she explained. Girls like her, who had scored well in both, were directed towards filling any available open slots for the benefit of the other girls who had excelled in only one area.

All of the slots for medicine were already filled.[ii]

"I wanted to be a doctor so much; I didn't know what else I could be!" she says, laughing. "I just supposed that if I couldn't be a doctor, surely, the next best thing must be a lawyer." And so, by chance more than ambition, Rachel headed for law school. She enrolled in Makerere University of Uganda, where she was one of only four women in a class of 29 students. After receiving her law degree, she worked for a local law firm as part of an apprentice program. Rachel enjoyed her first job as lawyer enough that she did not immediately suspect that she would change her career. That is, until she had a chance meeting with the representative of the UN High Commissioner for Refugees in Uganda. Rachel was awestruck. "I was so moved when the high commissioner's representative spoke about his work that I was inspired to pursue a similar path by working for the UN. My professor encouraged me to get a master's degree if working for the UN was something that I seriously wanted."

Fortunately, for Rachel, a scholarship program was available for students in Uganda who wanted to pursue advanced degrees abroad. Rachel applied for a master's program in law and was accepted at both Harvard and Oxford universities. Rachel had never been outside of Uganda until then and had no idea which school to choose. Torn between the two top schools, Rachel chose Harvard University. "The Oxford program was for two years and the Harvard program was only for one year... I wanted to return home as soon as possible." Rachel's father and mother, who enthusiastically supported their daughter's education, welcomed her decision to attend Harvard.

---

ii. Receiving good education was a key differentiating factor in Rachel's upbringing in Uganda. Illiteracy is still common in Uganda, particularly amongst women; more than one-third of Ugandan women were illiterate, as of 2002. This fact is exacerbated by high levels of poverty, with 35 percent of the population living below the international poverty line of US $1.25 per day, as of 2001 (CIA World Factbook, Uganda).

Encounter with the West

Rachel vividly remembers her first car ride with her host family through the city of Cambridge, Massachusetts, and in particular, the culture shock of seeing hippies for the first time. The year was 1972. "I thought to myself, 'Why aren't they wearing shoes? Can't they afford shoes?'" She laughs, remembering the naïveté of her youthful self. An even greater shock during those first few weeks in Cambridge was seeing "white men cleaning the streets." In Uganda, the only white men she ever saw were all in positions of power; it took time for her to adjust to the idea that white men, too, could work in the lower rungs of society.

Overall, her experience at Harvard was a great one. She loved the culture, the high quality of the education, and the people she met there. The school had a special program for foreign graduate students that enabled them to meet and socialize with cross sections of the student population, including first-year law students. Most importantly for Rachel, Harvard was where she met two of her best friends, one from the Netherlands and the other from Ghana. (Her best friend from Ghana, Sylvanus Tiewul, later became her husband.)

Rachel was firm in her desire to work for the UN and found that her two best friends also shared her passion; perhaps due to this shared passion, their friendship was able to deepen further. Rachel and her friends researched and spoke with professors to find out how they could work for the UN, carefully taking note of their advice on relevant courses to take. After much investigation, the three friends found that one of their professors had a contact in the UN Office of the Legal Counsel, just where Rachel hoped to find herself. With the professor's blessing, Rachel and her friends headed to New York City to meet with the legal counsel.

With expectations high, the trio had a promising first meeting with the legal counsel, who agreed to arrange for them to meet with the director of human resources at the UN. To them, it

*Addressing the Security Council, October 2009 /
UN Photo, Devra Berkowitz*

seemed that their dreams of working for the UN were about to come true. Hopeful and expectant, Rachel met individually with the director, as did her two friends. The director's reaction was not quite what she expected. The director was incredibly offended that Rachel had gone above her head rather than following the regular application procedure. The director argued that Rachel should have gone through the human resources office to search for job opportunities, not the legal counsel's office. None of them were hired. Lesson learned.

"Years later, when I was working for the UN—in the Office of Human Resources Management—I met the same director. I realized then that she was someone who took her job and the rules very seriously. She was doing what she believed was right." Now, as an experienced UN insider, Rachel sees the validity of the director's perspective. At the time, though, it was quite a setback, since Rachel was unfamiliar with UN procedures and had no idea what she was doing wrong. The trio returned to Cambridge, deflated from their meetings but still persistent in their desire to work for the UN.

After applying again, this time through official channels, the first of the three to be accepted for a position at the UN was Rachel's boyfriend, Sylvanus. Rachel smiles as she jokes, "It may have been a little easier for guys." Now inside the UN, Sylvanus was able to let her know as soon as there was an opening. Rachel applied for a temporary position in the Division for Equal Rights for Women within the Centre for Social Development and Humanitarian Affairs. This time, Rachel got the job and began what would prove to be a long, distinguished career at the UN. It was 1977.

Embarking on the UN Career

Following a short-term contract in the Division for Equal Rights for Women, Rachel got a full-time position as Special Assistant to the Assistant Secretary-General for Social Development and Humanitarian Affairs. In her new position, Rachel developed insights into social issues of concern to the international community and forged important contacts, a key to success in any setting. She was also actively involved in the establishment of the landmark Convention on the Elimination of Discrimination against Women. With her abilities and dedication recognized, Rachel was assigned to various posts in the UN system, including the Office of Human Resources Management and the Joint Appeals Board / Joint Disciplinary Committee.[iii]

Rachel subsequently joined the ranks of women pioneers who assumed new political and peacekeeping roles at the UN. She served in peacekeeping missions in Namibia from 1989 to 1990 (UN Transition Assistance Group)[iv] and in Iraq and Kuwait from

---

iii. The Joint Appeals Board considered UN staff appeals against administrative decisions, while the Joint Disciplinary Committee imposed disciplinary measures on staff that violated the UN Staff Rules. These mechanisms were replaced by the Office of Administration of Justice in July 2009.

iv. UN Transition Assistance Group (UNTAG) was established to assist the Special Representative of the Secretary-General to ensure the early independence of Namibia from South Africa through free and fair elections under the supervision and control of the UN (UNTAG website).

1992 to 1994 (UN Iraq-Kuwait Observer Mission).[v] Today, women constitute 3 percent of military personnel and 9 percent of police personnel out of approximately 110,000 peacekeepers.[5] However, in 1993, women made up only 1 percent of deployed uniformed personnel.[6] The mission in Namibia was no exception, and Rachel was thrown into an overwhelmingly male environment. Although she was an international civilian staff member in support of peacekeeping activities, her professionalism qualified her to be rated alongside women peacekeepers who had "proven that they can perform the same roles, to the same standards, and under the same difficult conditions as their male counterparts."[7]

In fact, her experience in Namibia—formerly known as South-West Africa—constitutes one of her most meaningful UN memories. At that time, South-West Africa had been under South African occupation since 1915, when German colonial administration ended with their defeat during World War I. When the supervisory authority over South-West Africa was transferred to the UN, South Africa refused to surrender its earlier League of Nations mandate and continued to illegally administer the country.[8] International pressures for independence mounted, and in 1966, the South West Africa People's Organization (SWAPO) began what turned into a decades-long armed struggle to liberate the country. This was followed by the renaming of South-West Africa into Namibia in 1968 and the UN recognition of SWAPO as the sole official representative of the Namibian people.[9]

In 1978, the Security Council adopted a resolution to settle the "Namibian problem." The resolution, known as the "UN Plan," called for holding elections in Namibia under UN supervision and control as well as cessation of all hostile acts by Namibian and South African troops, paramilitary, and police. Intense discussions between the concerned parties continued until 1988, when South

v. UN Iraq-Kuwait Observation Mission (UNIKOM) was established in April 1991, following the forced withdrawal of Iraqi forces from Kuwait. Its goals included monitoring the demilitarized zone along the Iraq-Kuwait border, deterring violations, and reporting on any hostile action (UNIKOM website).

Africa finally agreed to withdraw its presence and implement the UN Plan.

The transition to independence officially began in April 1989, and the United Nations Transition Assistance Group (UNTAG) arrived in Windhoek, the country's capital. Rachel was one of the 2,000 international civilian and local staff who joined the group[vi] and the only female in the management team. As indicated by the 19 fatalities during the mission's one year of operation, UNTAG faced many dangerous situations. However, Rachel was determined to make sure that her gender did not in any way delay or deter the mission's activities. She remembers a time when the team received intelligence that fighting had broken out near the electoral district they were visiting. Martti Ahtisaari of Finland, who would later become president of that nation, was heading the mission as a special representative of the secretary-general (1979–1990). He considerately asked Rachel to decide whether the team should return to the capital. Rachel decided they should stay, even though the military personnel warned "there were no separate accommodations for women." To Rachel, the Namibian mission was a place where women were allowed "to demonstrate their capabilities, competencies, and creativity" and showed "what they are capable of doing"[10]

Another inspiration that Rachel took away from Namibia was the leadership of Martti, which was characterized by "respect" for others. She recalls, "He was a big person -literally -quite a presence, with a big heart. He believed in bringing people together. He had respect for and was guided by the team." Over the years, Rachel found herself incorporating Martti's approaches to

---

vi. UNTAG's mission was to help achieve early independence of Namibia through free and fair elections. It also had to ensure that "all hostile acts were ended; troops were confined to base, and, in the case of the South Africans, ultimately withdrawn from Namibia; all discriminatory laws were repealed; political prisoners were released;Namibian refugees were permitted to return; intimidation of any kind was prevented; law and order were impartially maintained." Independent Namibia joined the UN in April 1990 (UNTAG website).

Consulting Under-Secretary-General for Peacekeeping Operations,
October 2006 / UN Photo, Devra Berkowitz

management. In particular, she has grown to believe that "respect for the individual and for one another is paramount... Many of the problems encountered at the workplace—such as harassment, sexual harassment, sexual exploitation—are really based on the lack of respect for others. If we all treat others as we would like them to treat us, I am sure that would go a long way to improving the work environment."[11]

After her successful performance in the peacekeeping missions, Rachel worked as Director of the Human Resources Management Division at the UN Food and Agriculture Organization (FAO) in Rome.[vii] According to Rachel, moving to FAO presented more challenges than she had anticipated due to its different organizational culture. She found FAO to be more centrally

vii. Founded in 1945, FAO's mandates are "to raise levels of nutrition, improve agricultural productivity, better the lives of rural populations, and contribute to the growth of the world economy," with special focus on developing rural areas, in which 70 percent of the world's poor and hungry people live (FAO website).

managed than the UN, as well as more fragmented in terms of staff representation. For example, general service staff, headquarters professional staff, and field professional staff at FAO each had a separate union, whereas in the UN Secretariat, all staff had one representative body.

Although it took time to adjust to these differences, Rachel was able to accomplish many things while at FAO, including the introduction of spouse employment, tele-working, and paternity leave. As a working mother of three young children, Rachel could understand the challenges of balancing work and life. Her innovative initiatives derived from both her own experience, as well as the experience of dealing with numerous single fathers or men who supported their spouses' careers by sharing family responsibilities. She wanted to create a work environment that not only promoted work and life balance but also fostered genuine gender equality in terms of entitlements.

In 2004, Rachel's hard work and dedication were rewarded when she was appointed Special Adviser of the Secretary-General on Gender Issues and Advancement of Women. Internally within the UN system, the special advisor is responsible for enhancing the status of women and mainstreaming gender issues[12] into the substantive work of the organization, which is broadly broken down to peace and security, development, human rights, humanitarian affairs, and international law. At the time of her appointment, Rachel remarked, "I am glad to return to the UN and complete a full circle as I am back to where my UN career started—working on gender issues." She noted that the position is different from other senior positions in the UN in that it is an "advocacy" position that requires speaking out on various issues that must be addressed.

As the special adviser, Rachel attached particular importance to empowering poor rural women in developing countries and preventing the trafficking of women and girls worldwide by giving them more viable economic opportunities. Another priority issue for Rachel was the landmark Security Council resolution 1325 on "women, peace, and security," which underlined the vital role of women in the prevention and resolution of conflicts. In October 2002, then Secretary-General Kofi Annan submitted a report as follow-up to the resolution "on the impact of armed conflict on women and girls, the role of women in peace-building, and the gender dimensions of peace processes and conflict resolution."[13] As the chair of the UN Inter-Agency Task Force on Women, Peace and Security,[viii] Rachel has concentrated on helping to implement the recommendations of the report to ensure that women become full partners in peace and security negotiations. In order to do so, she urged governments to establish "a comprehensive framework" that focuses on concrete goals and timeframe.[14] She observed, "More fundamentally, changes are required in the traditional perception of women as caregivers and caretakers rather than peacemakers. Investments are required in the educational sector to address and uproot prevailing stereotypes that lead to the exclusion of women from peace-building processes."[15]

Bringing her human resources background to bear, Rachel notes that effective personnel management is critical for the organization's optimal performance. Therefore, Rachel insists on holding managers accountable, while requesting them to give women the opportunities they deserve in an objective, transparent, and fair manner.[ix]

---

viii. Established in February 2001, the Inter-Agency Task Force on Women, Peace, and Security follows up on the implementation of the Security Council resolution 1325. It consists of 22 members from UN entities.

ix. The UN Charter established six principal organs of the UN: the General Assembly, the Security Council, the Economic and Social Council, the Trusteeship Council, the International Court of Justice, and the Secretariat. The UN family, however, is larger, encompassing 15 agencies and several programmes and bodies (UN website).

High Wire Balancing Act

Juggling work and life presented many challenges for Rachel, who was quickly rising through the ranks of the organization. It became apparent that having a spouse at the UN "can complicate one's life," and Rachel kept her maiden name to protect the couple's privacy. The couple also made a point of compartmentalizing work and family life. As a result, weekday lunch hours and evenings were set aside for work-related events; it was not unusual for the couple to sometimes go days without seeing their children, who would be sound asleep by the time they got home. The weekends, however, were strictly devoted to their children and their life together as a family. The heavy demands placed on them as working parents meant they had to do without personal "free hours" or entertainments, which New York City offered in abundance.

Although her husband did more than his share of housework and childcare, their frequent travel and work commitments made finding time for family, and for each other, difficult. Despite their best efforts to excel at both work and home, important things were sometimes forgotten. For example, due to the demands of their heavy schedules, Rachel and her husband had totally forgotten about a Parents' Day at their daughter's school, where young Tonia was performing in a play. They returned home in Long Island late that night, only to find their daughter crying miserably. With remorse still detectable in her voice, Rachel says, "I will never forget that. I still apologize to her for it. She was the only student without a parent. Now, as an adult, she always tells me, 'Forget about it, Mom, it's okay,' but I still haven't forgiven myself."

Balancing the conflicting demands of work and life became nearly impossible when tragedy unexpectedly struck the young family. When her first son was 13, second son 11, and her daughter 8, Rachel's husband, her best friend and colleague Sylvanus, died unexpectedly. It brought tremendous grief to the family, not least because he was so young and loving. The premature death of their father was extremely difficult for the children, as they were entering their teens when all sensitivities become heightened. Despite the emotional numbness that came from losing her husband, Rachel forced herself to cope by focusing on her children and did the best she could to blunt the ache of their growing up fatherless. Although her kids were young, they displayed an extraordinary amount of maturity in the face of adversity; they supported each other and

Meeting with former child soldiers from Uganda, November 2008 /
UN Photo, Ryan Brown

survived together. This approach gradually took root in the family. When there were problems, they would sit down together and discuss them, with everyone acting like a "juror."

"My children always check up on me," she says warmly. "Sometimes they'll say, 'Mom, why did you say that? We read in the news that you said such and such in a meeting.'" Rachel counts her children as her most honest critics and supporters and smiles when she recalls how her daughter would sometimes veto a scarf she had worn for a public photo. Rachel's oldest son studied business and is now involved in political work, while her youngest son majored in philosophy and is now working for a hedge fund.

Career discovery for her daughter, Tonia, came in a more tortuous way because of her multiple interests and talents and the infinite possibilities available for girls of her generation and background. Initially intent on becoming a writer, she changed her focus to law but is now attending medical school. Given Rachel's original childhood dream of becoming a doctor, her daughter's ultimate choice seems ironically fitting.

Aside from juggling work and family, Rachel found herself juggling her gender and age with her career aspirations and capabilities. She is quoted as saying, "As a black woman, I have felt discrimination so many times in my life on account of my combined race and gender. Moreover... many times I was told by my supervisors, 'You are too young, you can afford to wait for your promotion!' It is very offensive and presupposes that a woman is somehow flattered that she is 'young' and should therefore be happy to be denied an opportunity/ consideration. 'Time is on your side,' and this has followed me throughout my career. I have found this very insulting because, in the meantime, my male colleagues that entered the UN with me and looked just as young if not younger did not have to 'wait' to be promoted."[16] Rachel also confesses that some of the constraints she faced as a woman staff member came not only from men, but also from other women; however, she was determined not to be "hindered" by negative comments or actions, focusing instead on "[doing] what I was hired to do the best way I could."[17] Like an insightful psychologist, Rachel understands that "[d]iscriminatory treatment usually leads to insecurity, lack of confidence, and eventually affects the quality of work. Therefore, I have always made a conscious effort not to allow such conduct to destroy me."[18]

Rachel understands from experience that stereotypes such as "women are less able than men" still persist. Many women continue to find themselves having to do double the work to be proven the "same as men." Girls should not be discouraged by such double standards but work harder to change them. "Unfortunately, only when we are so much more capable than men and we accomplish so much more than them—only then can we convince the world that the two genders are genuinely equal." To Rachel, women still have a long way to go.

Looking Forward and Lessons Learned

Rachel is one of those rare individuals who have had the opportunity to develop her leadership skills very early in life. As the first daughter of nine siblings, Rachel had many occasions to make decisions, delegate responsibilities, and arbitrate squabbles. She attributes the foundation of her leadership skills to such childhood experience, which enabled her to learn firsthand how to manage different people in the confines of family hierarchy, social rules, and expectations.

As if she were counting off the letters of the alphabet, Rachel enumerates the essential qualities of a leader. "Great leaders are great listeners, with an appreciative heart. Leaders must know how to listen to the various voices of people, including their subordinates, and they must know how to demonstrate appreciation for others regardless of who they are and what their contributions. Active listening and active respect for each individual paves the way for a cohesive team." Rachel believes that leadership skills are developed through years of "conscious learning." Leadership is neither innately given nor acquired through technical training. It develops as part of the maturation process, through the people that you meet, and through the ordeals of life. Everyone has the potential to develop excellent leadership skills; the key is to identify and internalize those qualities that would help one grow as an individual.

In a multicultural setting like the UN, working with people whose beliefs and views are fundamentally different from one's own is inevitable. What is needed in this context is the willingness to accommodate diversity rather than impose a single standard.

This calls for consensus building, in which everyone in the team is involved and can freely share their ideas. Rachel admits that consensus building is challenging, as it takes much time and patience, but it appeals to her as the best method for leading successfully. However, she cautions that a decision-making process should always be driven by concrete vision to prevent derailing by endless debate.

Rachel makes a point of giving credit where it is due and generously compliments her staff when deserved. She believes in the power of encouragement as a motivator and uses it felicitously. As a result, she has seen many people improve their performance under her tutelage. "It takes confidence for people to perform optimally, and confidence only comes when their superiors acknowledge their contributions and cheer them on despite whatever weaknesses they may have." Further, being a leader also means remaining firm and standing by decisions. It is, of course, necessary to consult and engage diverse stakeholders before making decisions, but once decisions are made, they should be enforced. "I feel strongly about discipline and order. We have to stay in line once decisions are made. Anarchy is not an option." Her gentle appearance belies the firmness and adherence to order that makes her fearless about making tough decisions on issues that matter.

When asked how she handles criticism, Rachel replies that it is a necessary part of one's development. She always examines the basis for criticism in order not to repeat mistakes. However, on occasions when she believes that her words and actions are "right" or justified, Rachel approaches the criticizer directly. Sometimes wrongs are corrected and misunderstandings clarified, other times not, but the important thing is that through this attempt at dialogue, a degree of common ground is forged and civility maintained.

Rachel defines success in leadership as creating a motivated and happy team, where there is harmony. Only then can the team produce effectively and make an impact. Success in life, on the other hand, transports her away from the complexities of the UN to the simple joys of family life. Rachel feels successful because of her kids and the unbreakable bond they share together.

Rachel's job as a mother will never end, but she is anticipating retirement from the UN down the road. She has so many things that she wants to do afterwards that it hardly feels like it will be a retirement at all. Broadly, she wants to work with young women who are victims of violence, young girls who were kidnapped or sold to work the streets, and those who do not have choices in life because of poverty. Rachel wants to contribute to improving the lives of these women. Rachel recounts a story she read recently in a book by journalists Nicholas Kristof and Sheryl WuDunn called *Half the Sky: Turning Oppression into Opportunity for Women Worldwide* (2009). One of the stories in the book follows the life of a girl named Srey Momm in northwestern Cambodia, which is notorious for its many brothels. After working for five years in a brothel, Srey was "bought" by Nicholas for the paltry sum of $203. Nicholas intended to provide Srey the opportunity to start a new life; with Nicholas' financial help, Srey was able to start a meat stall in the market where her mother worked. However, after just one week, Momm voluntarily returned to the brothel because she was unable to overcome her addiction to methamphetamines. Apparently, brothel owners have administered this drug to keep their girls compliant and dependent. Srey was one of the countless girls snared in such a vicious scheme, unable to pull away despite her desire to do so.

Rachel agrees that, as with everything else, human rights work to save girls from unwilling prostitution is more complex than meets the eye. A more comprehensive "rescue package" is required to successfully transition girls to normal life. Rachel's dream is to create a global foundation that serves girls and women in due regard for their specific situations and cultural contexts. Rachel also wants to fundraise for women entrepreneurs who are struggling to reclaim their rightful positions in society. "There are women who work as maids for seven days a week under brutal conditions and girls who are married off when they are just entering their teens. All of them need our help. We must give them the opportunity to explore life and realize their potential." She looks back on her happy childhood and longs to provide to the world's girls the same kind of security and opportunity that were offered to her.

She recalls how in Saudi Arabia 15 schoolgirls died in a fire in 2002 because they were prevented from leaving the blazing building without wearing proper headscarves and abayas (black robes); in Afghanistan, little girls have been poisoned and killed for daring to go to school even after the Taliban's ban on female education (1996–2001) was lifted.[19] Such horrific stories leave her aching inside and reinforce her determination to fight the discrimination and bigotry that crushes the hopes and potential of so many girls. Rachel encourages young girls and women to determine what they would like to accomplish in life and go for it, to persevere and pursue their goals no matter how difficult. "Once they have their commitment, they shouldn't be deterred by occasional obstacles or disparaging remarks. If there are no challenges on the way, accomplishments may not be valuable."

In order to set and achieve a meaningful goal, Rachel declares, "First and foremost, one has to know oneself and be true to one's belief, which for me are 'perseverance' and 'the certainty that I am truly privileged'... This knowledge has obliged me to give and do my very best and keeps me going through my ups and downs and in all difficulties."[20] As a woman who has experienced both the good and bad of life in depth, Rachel has acquired the "wisdom in living life one day at a time, which is linked to planning." She advises, "Plan your life and be realistic about life, about what you can change and can't change. There is no point for me to keep banging my head against some door that won't open; instead, it is better to pursue those doors that are partially open. Maybe through them I can find a way into the other room... It is nice to be romantic about things, but we need not dwell too much on fantasies. We need to be well grounded and pursue our goals and use every opportunity to get to where we want to go."[21]

Finding Balance

Rachel shows us that, try as we might, we cannot always separate our career aspirations from the many other obstacles, disappointments, and obligations that appear in our lives. Life can be messy and difficult, but it can also be immensely rewarding.

Although it can be hard to find balance when times get tough, finding balance is a part of what makes leaders great — having the ability to truly hear and value diverse perspectives and needs, while simultaneously seeking to achieve one's purpose and vision in the face of life's challenges.

Authors' Note: On December 31, 2010, Rachel Mayanja retired from the United Nations after decades of dedicated service.

Patricia O'Brien

New York, 2009

Staying Positive

Patricia O'Brien

O n August 6, 2008, Patricia O'Brien was appointed by Secretary-General Ban Ki-moon as Under-Secretary-General for Legal Affairs and the UN Legal Counsel. She is the first woman to hold this position. According to the spokesperson for the secretary-general, who announced the appointment, Patricia "brings to the job an extensive experience of legal and international affairs, is eminently equipped to integrate the legal dimension in the internal decision-making processes, promote the rule of law in international relations, and contribute to ensuring an end to impunity."[1]

As head of the Office of Legal Affairs, Patricia oversees some 200 staff and a biennial budget of approximately $60 million. The overall objectives of the office are to 1) provide a unified central legal service for the Secretariat and the principal and other organs of the UN on questions of international and national, public, private, procedural, and administrative law; 2) contribute to the progressive development and codification of international public and trade law; 3) promote the strengthening, development, and effective implementation of the international legal order for the seas and oceans, namely the 1982 UN Convention on the Law of the Sea and related implementing Agreements; and 4) register and publish treaties, perform the depositary functions of the secretary-general, and provide assistance to member states in matters related to treaty law.[2]

Due to the nature of her job, Patricia works very closely with Secretary-General Ban Ki-moon, which gives her rare access to the man who is tasked with performing, in the words of the first Secretary-General Trygve Lie of Norway, "[T]he most impossible job on this earth." An example was a day in July, a month that tends to be slower than the other months on the UN calendar. Patricia tended to management issues in the morning, had a policy lunch with the secretary-general, and worked on substantive legal matters in the afternoon. At six o'clock, she gave a speech at the New York City Bar Association in celebration of the UN's International Justice Day. She then returned to the UN headquarters in the evening to meet with the secretary-general to deal with a pressing legal issue that had developed over the course of the day. When asked how she handles such a hectic schedule, Patricia answers, "Well, I wake up every day and start it as though it is my first day."

Patricia has a way of looking at things that is undeniably positive and sunny. When we meet her in her office, she quips that ever since her office was relocated to Madison Avenue— some six blocks away from the UN complex—as part of the building renovation plan, her trip to the headquarters has added a workout to her daily routine. Ms. O'Brien jovially points to her flat-soled shoe and commends it for transporting her back and forth on the forty-minute roundtrip without complaint — a much faster trip than trying to take a taxi across town in lunch hour traffic.

The Globetrotter Child

"Travel and independence came at a very young age for me," Patricia says. Of Irish descent, Patricia was born in 1957 in Brunei, officially the State of Brunei Darussalam, an Islamic country on the island of Borneo. (The third-largest island in the world, Borneo is located north of Australia in Southeast Asia, and is divided among Brunei, Indonesia, and Malaysia.)

At the time, Ireland was a relatively young country, having won its independence from the United Kingdom of Great Britain and Ireland (now the United Kingdom of Great Britain and Northern Ireland) in 1922. High levels of poverty and unemployment persisted, as did emigration, which began in massive scale during the Great Famine of the 1840s.[i] Until the 1950s, Ireland's economy essentially remained "a sector of the UK economy," with 90 percent of exports going to the UK and almost all imports coming from the UK.[3]

Patricia's father was a barrister, legal adviser, and managing director of Shell, a group of energy and petrochemicals companies with operations around the world. The second oldest and first daughter of four children, Patricia had since early childhood nurtured hopes of following in her father's footsteps and becoming a barrister. As for Patricia's mother, she raised the family, which was content to move to the various locations that their father's work took them.

In a childhood self-described as "peripatetic" or "nomadic," Patricia and her family moved frequently. When Patricia was two, the family left Brunei, subsequently spending seven years in Nigeria, four years in Cambodia, and four years in the Democratic Republic of Congo. Despite these constant relocations, Patricia never felt uprooted or out of place in the many countries that she lived thanks to her solid family support and happy childhood. A sort of social network that Patricia and her siblings built amongst themselves enabled them to adapt quickly to new environments and transformed what could have been disruptive and stressful events into fun adventure.

When Patricia was seven years old, she was sent to a boarding school in Ireland. As her childhood consisted of travelling and living life as a foreigner, it was a "strange" experience being placed in a boarding school where she was just another Irish girl. But she quickly adjusted to the environment with the social skills that she

i. Commonly known as the Irish Potato Famine, the Great Famine of 1845–1852 resulted in approximately one million deaths and the emigration of another million people, cutting Ireland's population by 20 to 25 percent.

had developed playing, squabbling, and growing up alongside her three siblings.

For the next ten years, Patricia would spend the academic year in Ireland and her summers abroad with her family, mostly in developing parts of the world. While her exposure to different peoples and cultures certainly affected Patricia's worldview and open perspective, it did not particularly disrupt or define who she was as a student making the most of her teenage years as a normal adolescent in Ireland. "When I was a teenager, I imagined I would be married and have a few children by the time I hit 30. I thought I would follow in my mother's footsteps, and assumed that 'housewife' was part of what I was supposed to be." Ironically, though, Patricia was always a high achiever, and at the age of 17, she enrolled in the prestigious Trinity College, Dublin, widely considered to be the best university in Ireland. There again, with her characteristic optimism and easy-going personality, she enjoyed a "good college life." However, her social success did not cause her academic life to take a backseat. While at Trinity, Patricia pursued two degrees, a bachelor of arts in legal science from Trinity College and a barrister-at-law from King's Inns, Dublin. She later earned a Master of Arts in 1987 from Trinity College.

Patricia, fourth from right, with members of the Office of Legal Affairs' Treaty Section at the Annual Treaty Event, September 2010

Patricia's drive towards high achievement was largely self-motivated. Her parents were very committed to providing the highest standards of education, but never pressured their children to excel academically or to pursue specific professional careers. Her parents were "there" for Patricia when she needed encouragement, guidance, and support but did not force her in any particular direction. Her career path was hers to decide, as was her younger brother Paul's, who also coincidentally chose to study law. A Harvard-trained lawyer with years of experience in developing countries, including Afghanistan and Kenya, Paul O'Brien is currently the Vice President of Policy and Advocacy at Oxfam America, also making a difference in the international public arena.

Woman with a White Wig

For her first job out of college, Patricia was self-employed as a barrister in Dublin. In Ireland, one becomes a barrister after completing three rigorous stages: academic (obtaining an approved law degree); vocational (passing an entrance examination and undertaking a one-year degree of barrister-at-law at the Honorable Society of King's Inns,[ii] the only institution in the country with the mandate to provide training courses and confer degrees for barristers); and a one-year apprenticeship stage. A candidate is then admitted to practice by the Chief of Justice of Ireland, and spends an additional year in non-paid "pupilage" or "deviling" under an approved Dublin-based practitioner. With that, an aspiring barrister becomes a member of the Law Library, following which he or she can finally take up one's own work and start building up a practice.

When Patricia qualified for the Irish Bar, she was in her early twenties and her father had just passed way. It was a difficult

---

ii. Established in 1541, King's Inns is the oldest institution of professional legal education in Ireland, with the sole capacity to call individuals to the bar and to disbar them.

transition, to say the least. As a self-employed barrister, Patricia had to find a way to establish her career without the cushion of a regular salary or stable employment, as being a barrister in Ireland involved building one's own practice from scratch. It took about two years to build a stable and growing practice on her own. During this time, Patricia focused on "making a living" and did not let her situation overwhelm her.

Fortunately, she benefited from a supportive Irish Bar, a "wonderful experience," as she puts it. She recalls the anachronism of wearing the white wigs and elaborate gowns characteristic of the institution. The year was 1979, and she was one of about ten women out of roughly 400 barristers.[iii] Despite these seemingly troubling numbers, Patricia never felt discriminated against because of her gender. It was actually "fine being a woman" at the Irish Bar. On the contrary, she thought that the men at the Bar were "subtly protective" of her, a reality she acknowledges was "unusual." "Perhaps it was because they didn't really see me as a threat," she conjectures.

As a young woman, she faced certain expectations that she should focus on family law, "helping wives who were abused by husbands," for example. But Patricia allowed herself to examine and pursue her true interests, and offered herself an opportunity to do very interesting and diverse work, ranging from commercial, constitutional, and criminal law to extensive advocacy and opinion writing. She stayed at the Irish Bar for almost a decade.

Paving the Way to the UN

During this time, Patricia met her former husband, an Irish psychiatrist who was on visit in Ireland from Vancouver, Canada. Although Patricia had always intended to marry early, she actually ended up getting married when she was 30. Patricia recalls, "I

---

iii. As of October 2010, there are 2,311 members of the Law Library, with 60 percent male and 40 percent female.

wasn't resisting marriage. I put equal value to family and career. It just happened that way." In 1988, after nine years at the Irish Bar, Patricia packed up everything to follow her heart and her husband. Patricia moved to Vancouver, where she lived with her husband and their three young children for the next eight years. During this time, she taught part-time at the University of British Columbia and also qualified for the Canadian Bar. Despite these accomplishments, Patricia admits that her career was not really her focus during that period. "My focus was always on our three children."

The marriage, unfortunately, did not last. The couple divorced in 1996, after which Patricia and her three children moved back to Ireland. As a single mother, Patricia needed to find a way to support her family that would enable them to have immediate stability. She knew that if she returned to the Irish Bar, she would have to start her practice from scratch all over again; therefore, she needed to find another way to practice law.

By "luck or fortuitousness or serendipity"— although Patricia concedes that these words do not do justice to the hard work she put in — she quickly found a job as a civil servant at the Office of the Attorney General, providing legal services to the Irish government.

After demonstrating intensive drive and legal expertise, Patricia was appointed as legal counselor at the Irish Permanent Representation to the European Union in Brussels in 1998. In this capacity, she advised the government of Ireland on matters of European law and in legal proceedings before the International Court of Justice, the European Court of Human Rights, and the European Court of Justice. She subsequently served as legal adviser to the Department of Foreign Affairs of Ireland, starting in 2003. Patricia describes herself at the time as "an outsider" vis-à-vis the UN. She was "from a small but committed Member State, looking in on how this vast and complex body worked," getting only "a fleeting glimpse at most of the issues, or, for a very concentrated focus on an issue of particular national importance."

Nevertheless, she developed a real interest in the UN and in matters of public international law and started building a solid profile in this area.

The positions that she held as a "legal" diplomat would serve her well in her future at the UN, as they required a high level of political acumen. During these years, Patricia not only had to teach herself comprehensively about foreign policy issues, but also had to learn the ropes of politics, both domestic and international. Some of the hot button issues that she dealt with included terrorism, abortion, freedom of expression, extradition, and problems related to Northern Ireland. Representing a predominantly Catholic country in abortion cases proved particularly challenging, as she had to be sensitive to the sentiments of the Irish public—85 percent of which is Roman Catholic.

Other memorably difficult issues pertained to negotiating the Charter of Fundamental Rights of the European Union, which was signed and proclaimed by the presidents of the European Parliament at the European Council Meeting in Nice, France, on December 7, 2000. The charter sets out the whole range of civil, political, economic, and social rights of all European citizens and residents. As such, agreeing on a text that was acceptable to all negotiating parties required much corridor diplomacy, individual consultations, and strategic compromise.

In her subsequent career as a civil servant, and with her professional status and responsibilities growing by the day, what proved most challenging (and most rewarding) was the task of raising her children as a single mother. Throughout Patricia's life, her mother has been an extraordinary support. She provided the stability and security for Patricia to raise her children. Because Patricia knew that she could not spend as much physical time with her children as stay-at-home moms, she made every effort to impress upon her children that they would always be her number-one priority, regardless of whether she was at home or away. They could always reach her when needed, and Patricia believes that, as a result, they were able to grow up into the positive individuals that they are today.

Patricia beams when she talks about her children. "My eldest daughter is studying medicine in Dublin. My son, the middle one, is majoring in history and economics at Trinity College, Dublin, my alma mater. My youngest daughter is studying law, also at Trinity." While she appreciates that her children are proud of her professional accomplishments, she regrets that she missed many of the details of their young lives due to her attention to her work. Recently her daughter said, "Mom, I'm going to test your knowledge as a mother. What is my confirmation name?"[iv] Much to her embarrassment, Patricia could not remember it.

Today, Patricia makes a conscious effort to spend as much time as possible with her children. Her experience with her children has shaped her perspective on what is most important in life. She appreciates her career and is excited about her work, but she also places a high value on her relationships. Her children are very important to her and have taught her that there is more to life than career.

Another cherished relationship in Patricia's life is with her partner, Conor Quigley, whom she met twelve years ago in Stockholm. They enjoy many mutual interests. He is a barrister based in London, a Queen's Counsel, who specializes in European Law. They have tried to spend as much time together over the years as possible with Conor travelling back and forth to Dublin, Brussels, and now, to and from New York. This makes the time spent together and with the children even more precious, as it is never for very long at a stretch. Despite the distances between them, Patricia says Conor's support has been constant and unwavering and that their "wonderful relationship works beautifully."

---

iv. A rite of initiation in Catholicism in which the initiate receives a "confirmation name," usually the name of a saint whom that person admires or feels a special closeness with.

First Female Legal Counsel at the UN

Patricia's transition from barrister at the Irish Bar to under-secretary-general at the UN was facilitated by her longstanding interest in public international law, which developed at Trinity College. Like many young people around the world, Patricia had an "undefined" interest in the UN; when she mentioned her interest to her tutor at Trinity College, he encouraged her to "go out there and get more experience." And so she did.

With Secretary-General Ban Ki-moon, Los Angeles, March 2010

After decades of her active presence in the international legal field, Patricia's knowledge and competence were widely recognized. Several delegates and UN staff encouraged her to apply for the position of UN legal counsel when her predecessor was leaving. It was perhaps "fortuitous" that she previously served as a legal adviser to her government, for Patricia recounts that "[this UN] position is sometimes filled by legal advisers to foreign ministries, because they practice public international law on a daily basis."[6]

Patricia went through an arduous interview process, including an in-depth meeting with Secretary-General Ban Ki-moon. After careful consultation amongst the interview panel, she was offered the position, a decision heartily endorsed and welcomed by the Irish Department of Foreign Affairs. Patricia readily reveals that she is "very honored and proud" to be the organization's first female legal chief, not only for its significance, but for helping to inspire some of the women she has met.

Patricia notes that while she does not forget that she is "the first woman" to be legal counsel, the secretary-general's respect goes far beyond the gender element. "His commitment to gender equality has certainly helped me as the first woman in this role. He sees us as professionals. He always interacts with his staff as professionals and completely without gender bias." Patricia highly regards the secretary-general's commitment to gender equality. "He practices as he preaches," she says.

Besides launching many initiatives on gender issues, including the campaign on Say No — UNiTE to End Violence against Women, his leadership has catalyzed UN member states to adopt a decision on the establishment of UN Women, UN Entity for Gender Equality and the Empowerment of Women in 2010. Patricia has been working closely with Deputy Secretary-General Asha-Rose Migiro to lay the legal foundation for this new body. To Patricia, it is an honor and much fun to work with leaders so dedicated to causes that she believes in.

Being a principal legal adviser to the UN, the Office of Legal Affairs carries out much of its work "quietly and behind the scenes." The issues dealt with by the office range from peacekeeping operations and international criminal justice to the new system of Administration of Justice for a staff of more than 60,000.[v] Specific tasks include drafting rules of engagement for UN troops in dangerous situations, assisting member states in the negotiation of treaties and international legal texts, and advising on multimillion-dollar procurement contracts. All these are intended to uphold the UN Charter, in which the peoples of the UN expressed their determination "to establish conditions under which justice and

v. The Office of the Administration of Justice was established in July 2009, following the 2007 General Assembly resolution, which called for more effective handling of internal disputes and disciplinary matters in the UN.

respect for the obligations arising from the treaties and other sources of international law can be maintained." Patricia believes that international law—and the role of the UN as its champion—is "absolutely central"[7] to the work of the UN and to the secretary-general, and places emphasis on ensuring that international law and jurisprudence are continually advanced. She is convinced of the secretary-general's commitment to international law.

Due to its involvement in all aspects of the organization's work, the Office of Legal Affairs has enormous workload and pressure. Patricia is quick to pay tribute to the enormous commitment of the office's staff to the success of its work and reputation. Patricia places priority on the health of the office and its personnel, which mostly consist of experienced lawyers, many of whom have dedicated their careers to working in the UN system, with some who have joined from the private and academic sectors. Patricia wants her team to work together in a manner similar to the Senior Management Group, which consists of 36 UN senior managers who promote coherence and transparency through constant information flow and coordination. In addition to doing legal work they are also "expected to manage," because without proper management, they cannot achieve efficiency. Patricia herself spends a lot of time on management, setting goals, speaking with her staff and evaluating their outputs, and monitoring the office budget. She finds regularly communicating with her staff to be an especially important way of ensuring that they are assigned to the most suitable tasks to most efficiently achieve their shared objectives.

As legal counsel, Patricia attends many policy meetings chaired by the secretary-general, including the Senior Management Group. These policy meetings, which require her input and attendance, occur on "a frequent basis," since issues under the purview of her mandate are essentially limitless, running the gamut of public international law to UN administration and management. "Discussions at all the secretary-general's meetings, as you might

At a meeting at United Nations headquarters, 2010

imagine, are lively and sometimes difficult. As chair, the secretary-general works to ensure that the focus remains firmly on his goals for the organization."[8] Through these discussions, feelings of shared objectives and solidarity are enhanced, and managers get a better understanding of how the organization works and where it is headed.

As is expected, given the diverse backgrounds, perspectives, and personalities of each senior manager, it is practically impossible to build full consensus and obtain buy-in for all of the secretary-general's initiatives and programs. There are bound to be people who remain unhappy with the work of the secretary-general and his team.

For Patricia, however, it is clear that the secretary-general is very effective and is an extraordinarily committed and hard-working chief. She says that his fundamental humility and honor as a man shine through on a daily basis. She states, "The secretary-general places a particular emphasis on the need to reform the administration of the UN and to manage the resources of the organization as effectively as possible, including minimizing duplication and overlap. He does all this with one goal in mind: to enable the UN to perform its important mandates, in particular, the maintenance of international peace and security."[9]

International Law in Practice

As the only organization in the world that has universal membership, legitimacy, and global presence, the UN juggles dual functions; it enables world leaders to convene and set norms, such as the Millennium Development Goals,[vi] and it performs "legwork" to translate these norms into reality.

One of the key norms that the organization strives to advance is rule of law. Rule of law is driven by the principle that "everyone is accountable to the law—from the individual to the state itself." She believes that rule of law is "fundamental and essential" to preventing conflict, maintaining peace, protecting human rights, and sustaining economic development.

Another important part of Patricia's work pertains to fighting impunity for the perpetrators of genocide, crimes against humanity, and war crimes. Although international criminal mechanisms have brought to justice many who had planned and directed serious crimes in the conflicts of Rwanda, the former Yugoslavia, Sierra Leone, Cambodia, and elsewhere, many more have escaped, and their victims are rarely granted redress. To Patricia, it is highly

---

vi. Building upon a decade of major UN conferences and summits, world leaders gathered at UN headquarters in New York in September 2000 and committed their nations to collectively achieve eight Millennium Development Goals (MDGs) by 2015 "to realize [their] universal aspirations for peace, cooperation, and development." The MDGs aim to 1) eradicate extreme poverty and hunger; 2) achieve universal primary education; 3) promote gender equality and empower women; 4) reduce child mortality; 5) improve maternal health; 6) combat HIV/AIDS, malaria and other diseases; 7) ensure environmental sustainability; and 8) develop a global partnership for development.

important that peace processes to end armed conflicts move in parallel with processes to bring justice to perpetrators of serious international crimes during these conflicts. She declares, "Without peace, justice would be difficult to achieve; and without justice, peace could be difficult to sustain."

Looking Forward and Lessons Learned

Despite her many successes, Patricia is not without failures and disappointments. She had faced difficulties and challenges as a young barrister, working to build her own practice, as well as many challenges raising her children alone after the end of her marriage. Patricia's strength lay with the fact that she simply chose to focus on the successes and the possibilities for her future, rather than the failures and disappointments.

Patricia admits that "setbacks are part of life," and when things go wrong, she always tries to examine the reasons but not to dwell on the negative. She applies the same principle to criticisms. Although the Office of Legal Affairs is generally less exposed to media scrutiny than other UN entities (due to its role as a dispenser of legal advice rather than an agenda-setter or policymaker), criticism of her office is still a reality that must be dealt with. After she examines and does her best to extract lessons from these criticisms, Patricia lets them go, not only because many of them can be quite hurtful, but because she truly believes that "a better future is based on learning lessons and moving forward." This is not to say that one should deny or intentionally forget the past, but rather to emphasize that dwelling on the past can undermine one's future by preventing one from seeing the opportunities and possibilities that lie ahead.

Patricia believes that young people should always remember to believe in themselves and to know that the future can be brighter than they had imagined. "Never doubt your ability to achieve more than what you thought possible," she says. For Patricia, some of her achievements were driven by necessity. Unexpectedly becoming a single mother required her to rely on herself and to work hard so that she could make a decent living for her three children.

That being said, her experience taught her that it is not always in one's best interest to focus solely on career. Patricia believes that sometimes focusing too hard on professional life can be detrimental to one's sense of fulfillment. It takes time to discover what matters most in life, and what matters most differs for each individual. Therefore, simply following a one-ingredient recipe for success and career advancement is not necessarily the best path to happiness. Perhaps this outlook was also shaped by the fact that her parents did not push her to be an overachiever. In fact, Patricia's mother always tells her, "You work too hard."

Focusing on more than just career is one way to protect one's self against the many external changes of one's life. Life does not always turn out to be what one thinks or hopes, and it may be tougher to handle should things go in an unexpected direction. "I can say with confidence that I did not focus on building a career profile that would land me at this or that position," Patricia says. And yet, she has managed to achieve so much in her career, even becoming the UN's first female legal counsel. Though she is proud of her achievements, these achievements were not requirements for her to feel that she has lived and is living a happy and fulfilled life.

Before we leave our meeting with her, Patricia shares with us the one thing that she believes matters most: "I do the job that is given to me to the best of my ability."

Patricia has a simple, yet rich vision for her life after retirement from the UN. Years from now, when she has left her high-profile position, Patricia foresees herself living simply at home, surrounded by her family, including, hopefully, a handful of grandchildren, as well as her books and a pretty garden. As a lover of academic environments and intellectual stimulation, she could also see herself, book in hand, getting ready to teach a young generation of law students.

Staying Positive

Patricia shows us that maintaining a positive attitude in the face of life's challenges is an approach that can serve us well, whether we are evaluating our personal or professional lives. Perhaps it is this positive attitude that enabled the many seemingly "serendipitous" events in Patricia's life to occur. By letting go of the past and focusing herself firmly on her future, her eyes were open to those chances and opportunities that others might have simply passed by.

Sharing the Light

"And as we let our own light shine, we unconsciously give other people permission to do the same"
— Marianne Williamson, A Return to Love: Reflections on the Principles of "A Course in Miracles"

Whether or not we find ourselves in the public arena, as the women in this book have, the fact remains that society will always have expectations about who we are as women and who we should be. These expectations can range from how daughters should behave and when they should get married to what sectors women should work in, if at all.

At some point, we must all ask ourselves how we will respond to the expectations of our culture and upbringing. In some cases, our responses will be shaped by the examples of the women we see around us. In others, our responses may be determined by a desire to embark on a path that those around us have never taken before.

When we began interviewing the five women in this book, we had no way of knowing just how diverse their personal life experiences would be. We knew that they came from very different cultural and ethnic backgrounds — Sri Lanka, Germany, Argentina, Uganda, and Ireland — and that these backgrounds would likely have influenced how they grew up, their expectations for their own lives, and their perspectives on the world. But we soon found that there were also vast differences in family circumstances, ranging from working-class neighborhoods to elite boarding schools to an only child to the oldest daughter out of nine children.

Although the details and circumstances of their lives leading up to their positions with the UN are incredibly varied, throughout each story we found several commonalities that enabled each woman to overcome societal expectations and to take control of her life in an empowered way. These commonalities include a love of learning and access to a high-quality education, the ability to overcome personal obstacles, a willingness to remain open to new possibilities, an inward-focused definition of success, and a sense of humility.

Without exception, a love and respect for learning and access to a high-quality education served as a catalyst for opening up a world of possibilities for all of the women featured in this book. As Angela Kane's mother told her when she was growing up, an education is one thing that no one can take away from you. Although Angela's small-town German roots and her mother's stay-at-home example would have had many people predict that she would lead a simple, married life close to where she grew up, Angela's education took her far beyond the world that was familiar to her. First, it was to Munich for university — a chance to study in the big city. Then, it was Bryn Mawr College — her first time abroad. Finally, her academic excellence allowed her to secure a position with renowned organizations like the World Bank and the UN, where she had the opportunity to travel the globe, experience different cultures, and contribute to the unfolding of history through peacemaking and international public management.

For Rachel Mayanja, securing a position with the UN had its early beginnings with her childhood experience of studying at a prestigious boarding school for daughters of Uganda's ruling class. This advantage provided the building blocks for her academic excellence at the University of Makerere, followed by a scholarship to Harvard Law School. Through Rachel's shining example of how far an education can take a girl and how much that girl can later do for the world, we come to realize the urgency of providing educational opportunities to every girl in the world. The failure to cultivate these young minds prevents all of us from reaping the benefits of the creative potential of all of humanity. This drives home the importance of ensuring that all children receive a quality education that would equip them to take advantage of life's varied opportunities.

The high-quality education that Radhika, Angela, Susana, Rachel, and Patricia received empowered them to create their paths as they saw fit, allowing them to be self-sufficient and bold in their decision making at both personal and professional levels. The quality of these women's educations acted as a kind of alchemic force in their lives, capable of transforming any potentially limiting expectations or obstacles into valuable lessons or professional opportunities.

Although each of these women experienced judgments and pressure on how they should or should not lead their lives, their knowledge and capabilities put them in the driver's seat, with the ability to go as far as their own resilience and self-belief would allow. For Angela Kane, following her passions often put her in situations where the worth of her work as a woman was questioned; she was even told to consider volunteering rather than becoming a full-time employee since she was, after all, married. Rather than lose her composure, these experiences taught her to remain firm in her determination, which in turn caused those around her to change their preconceived notions about what she could do as a woman.

Radhika Coomaraswamy braved the cultural and familial pressures that come with being a South Asian woman, and made her passion for children and women's rights her life's priority. At the price of staying true to her beliefs, she had to endure the type of vicious public attacks reserved only for those brave enough to stand up to those in power who have committed acts of injustice. In so doing, she developed a commitment to truth that has positively impacted the lives of many people around the world.

In some cases, the level of difficulty that these women experienced extended to the realm of deep personal tragedy, forcing them to grow in inner strength and determination. Rachel Mayanja encountered devastation early in her career at the UN when her loving husband died unexpectedly. Faced with raising three children on her own, she found a way to maintain her sense of professionalism, continuing to advance in her career at the UN while also fostering an unbreakable bond with her children that has lasted into their adulthood.

Patricia O'Brien similarly experienced the challenge of raising three children after her divorce. To make the best of the situation, Patricia tapped into her legal talents and resourcefulness, teaching herself much of what she needed to know to become a respected legal mind in the international public sector and set the stage for her ascent as the first female legal counsel of the UN. Her optimism about her life enabled her to handle difficult circumstances with grace, which further contributed to the realization of her goals, both old and new. Like Rachel, Patricia forged a strong bond with her children, which she counts as one of the best blessings of her life.

Our interviews with these women showed us that oftentimes life throws things at us that we never expected that we would have to deal with. The path is not always easy, but that certainly does not mean that it's impossible. Our willingness and resilience to carry on in the face of obstacles big and small is what can make the difference between a life fulfilled and a life half lived.

By the same token, life sometimes presents things that we never expected or dreamed we would have the opportunity to receive. Being open and ready to recognize these opportunities is a major factor in creating new possibilities out of difficult circumstances. When Susana Malcorra left Telecom Argentina at the height of the financial crisis, she did not consider herself to be a failure. While it was difficult to see the company that she had led file for bankruptcy, she took the experience as an opportunity to completely reinvent herself. She realized that her skills could be put to good use in a myriad of other sectors and, with her sense of compassion, discovered a new calling in the international public arena.

A sense of openness to new opportunity undoubtedly played a role in where these women are today. Although each of the women we introduced in this book made it to a position of power at the UN, not one of them was entirely certain from the beginning exactly where her career would go. When the representative of the High Commissioner for Refugees visited Uganda, Rachel Mayanja was so moved by his words and passion that she opened herself up to the possibility of using her law degree in a way that would serve human rights in the international community.

Each of these women allowed their passion and conscience to dictate the course of their careers and found that in trusting their hearts and instincts, they were able to achieve success, sometimes in unexpected ways. But what exactly is success? How do we define it and how do we attain it? Rather than seeking success in outward recognition or status, each of the women we interviewed saw the true barometer of her success as measured by the sense of fulfillment she felt internally. As Susana Malcorra explained to us, it's possible to feel very successful or like a complete failure while being in the exact same professional position. What this tells us is that success is a subjective concept that can only truly be defined by the person experiencing it. Simply having a coveted title, which garners praise, recognition, and sometimes wealth, is not necessarily what makes one successful.

When Radhika Coomaraswamy was graced with the title of "Deshamanya" by the president of Sri Lanka, she was both humbled and surprised. She was surprised because she did not view herself as someone who would receive such an honor from the government whose human rights records she had criticized on a regular basis. She had prided herself on her willingness to stand up to authority, to speak out her true beliefs, even if it went against the status quo, and never expected that the government would recognize her work.

Although these titles and honors are wonderful rewards for years of hard work and dedication, they are, at the end of the day, simply "things." Just as the world can grace you with titles and honors when you are at the top of your game, so too can the world take those honors away, instead giving you harsh criticism and attacks. Given the whimsical nature of external symbols of failure or success, the women we interviewed decided that it was up to them to determine the parameters of a "successful life" and up to them to create it. In some cases, this meant balancing family and professional life; in others this meant focusing one's passion on career, and in others this meant finding a way to reinvent oneself in the face of adversity.

Crucial to this type of reinvention is the conviction that tomorrow will be different from yesterday. Patricia O'Brien's ability to focus firmly on the future and all of its possibilities enabled her to meet today's challenges with optimism, despite the day's daunting realities. Rachel Mayanja also maintained the philosophy "to live one day at a time" to the best of one's abilities in the certainty that what tomorrow brings depends on what one does today. While facing personal and professional challenges many would deem devastating, both Patricia and Rachel managed to build upon those challenges to achieve greater success as mothers and as professionals. Such resilience enabled all of the women we profiled to keep moving forward, expecting, willing, and working towards better things to come.

All of these women admit that even though they made it to a position in life where they feel a degree of success, there still remains much work to be done. Beyond managing the day to day responsibilities of their office, they spend much time on managing themselves, a task that is hugely important for any professional, particularly one in a position of power. One must have the vision and insight to do what one believes is best, making difficult decisions where necessary, while also valuing the viewpoints of others. As Angela Kane explained to us, this requires having confidence in one's own capabilities combined with the humility to acknowledge others' contributions without a sense of wounded pride. Self-confidence and expertise enable a manager to make tough decisions and to stand by them. And, as Susana Malcorra discovered when joining the international civil service after spending decades in the private sector, this also requires the ability to use one's capabilities under complex circumstances where the objectives are sometimes unclear and the stakeholders politically sensitive.

The process of meeting and learning about these exceptional women taught us that it really doesn't matter how you begin. After all, all of the women we profiled, now in positions of power at the UN, were once young girls born to families big and small, from towns rural and cosmopolitan, in regions all over the world. Rather, it's the choices and the efforts you make that will take you far, choices to carry on and not give up and to do those things that make you light up inside—these make all of the difference in how the story unfolds. If you are then fortunate enough to attain a position of power and are fulfilled and successful on your path, you must share that light with others and be humble enough to see their light as well.

Notes

At a Glance: United Nations

1. Ziring, Lawrence, Robert Riggs, and Jack Plano. *The United Nations: International Organization and World Politics* (Belmont, California: Wadsworth, 2005), p. 24.
2. Ibid., p. 39.

At a Glance: United Nations and Women

1. Economic and Social Council resolution, E/RES/2/11 (21 June 1946).
2. Global Issues, United Nations website (accessed January 2011).
3. Short History of the Commission on the Status of Women, UN Women website. (http://www.un.org/womenwatch/daw/CSW60YRS/CSWbriefhistory.pdf)
4. Ibid.
5. Ibid.
6. Ziring, Lawrence, Robert Riggs, and Jack Plano. *The United Nations: International Organization and World Politics* (Belmont, California: Wadsworth, 2005).
7. Jain, Devaki. *Women, Development, and the UN: A Sixty-year Quest for Equality and Justice* (Bloomington: Indiana University Press, 2005), p. 46.
8. Ibid., p. 35-36.
9. Quoted in Jain, Devaki. *Women, Development, and the UN: A Sixty-year Quest for Equality and Justice* (Bloomington: Indiana University Press, 2005), p. 55.
10. Mayanja, Rachel. Opening remarks delivered at the Fifth International Helvi Sipilä Seminar (New York, 4 March 2010).
11. General Assembly resolution, A/RES/3010.
12. Jain, Devaki. *Women, Development, and the UN: A Sixty-year Quest for Equality and Justice* (Bloomington: Indiana University Press, 2005), p. 67.
13. General Assembly resolution, A/RES/3520.
14. Short History of the Commission on the Status of Women, UN Women website.

15. Ibid.
16. Fasulo, Linda. *An Insider's Guide to the UN.* (New Haven: Yale University Press, 2009).
17. Short History of the Commission on the Status of Women, UN Women website.
18. Convention on the Elimination of All Forms of Discrimination against Women, UN Women website (accessed January 2011).
19. Quoted in Jain, Devaki. *Women, Development, and the UN: A Sixty-year Quest for Equality and Justice* (Bloomington: Indiana University Press, 2005), p. 81.
20. Short History of the Commission on the Status of Women, UN Women website.
21. Outcomes on Gender and Equality, UN website (accessed January 2011).
22. Ibid.
23. Short History of the Commission on the Status of Women, UN Women website.
24. Jain, Devaki. *Women, Development, and the UN: A Sixty-year Quest for Equality and Justice* (Bloomington: Indiana University Press, 2005).
25. Millennium Development Goals, UN website.
26. Jain, Devaki. *Women, Development, and the UN: A Sixty-year Quest for Equality and Justice* (Bloomington: Indiana University Press, 2005).
27. ECOSOC conclusion 1997/2.
28. World Summit outcome, A/RES/60/1 (September 2005), paragraph 116.
29. Study submitted by the United Nations Secretary-General on Women, Peace and Security (2002), p. 31.

Radhika Coomaraswamy

1. United Nations International School website (accessed December 2010).
2. Malhotra, Anju, and Amy O. Tsui. "Marriage Timing in Sri Lanka: The Role of Modern Norms and Ideas." *Journal of Marriage and Family* 58.2 (May 1996).
3. Ibid.
4. De Alwis, Malathi. "The Changing Role of Women in Sri Lankan Society." Social Research 69.3 (Fall 2002).
5. Coomaraswamy, Radhika. Statement delivered at the *World Conference Against Racism, Racial Discrimination, Xenophobia, and Related Intolerance* (Durban, September 2001).
6. Coomaraswamy, Radhika. "The Protection of Women and Children during Armed Conflict: Whose Responsibility," 2007 Chancellor's Human Rights Lecture delivered at the University of Melbourne (Melbourne, 13 December 2007).
7. Human Rights Commission of Sri Lanka website (accessed December 2010).
8. Center for Education of Women Newsletter. University of Michigan (Spring 2009).
9. United Nations News Centre (31 July 2009).
10. Coomaraswamy, Radhika. "The Protection of Women and Children during Armed Conflict: Whose Responsibility," 2007 Chancellor's Human Rights Lecture delivered at the University of Melbourne (13 December 2007).
11. United Nations News Centre (31 July 2009).
12. United Nations *Women's Newsletter* 10.2 (April, May, June 2006).

Angela Kane

1. UN Secretariat website (accessed December 2010).
2. UN Department of Management website (accessed December 2010).
3. UN website "Reform at the United Nations" (accessed December 2010).
4. Statistisches Bundesamt Deutschland website (accessed January 2011).
5. UN Department of Public Information. SG/A/1135 (13 May 2008).
6. Ibid.
7. Ban, Ki-moon. Transcript of press conference in Norway, UN website (31 August 2009).

Susana Malcorra

1. *Encyclopedia Britannica*, "Rosario."
2. *CIA — The World Factbook: Argentina.*
3. Ibid.
4. Ibid.

Rachel Mayanja

1. Background Note on Uganda. *United States Department of State* website (accessed January 2011).
2. Country Study on Uganda. *United States Library of Congress* (1991).
3. United Nations *Women's Newsletter* 8.3 (July, August, September 2004).
4. Ibid.
5. United Nations Peacekeeping website (accessed January 2011).
6. Ibid.
7. Ibid.
8. Background Note on Uganda. *United States Department of State* website (accessed January 2010). Country Study on Uganda. *United States Library of Congress* (1991).
9. United Nations Peacekeeping website (accessed January 2011).
10. United Nations *Women's Newsletter* 8.3 (July, August, September 2004).
11. Ibid.
12. Ibid.
13. United Nations Security Council resolution 1325, paragraph 16 (31 October 2000).
14. Mayanja, Rachel. "Ensuring Women's Participation in Peacekeeping" delivered at the Tenth Anniversary of Security Council Resolution 1325 at the European Union (Brussels, 9 September 2010).
15. Ibid.
16. Ibid.
17. Ibid.
18. Ibid.
19. Qazi, Abdullah. "The Plight of the Afghan Woman," Afghanistan Online (9

December 2010).

20. United Nations *Women's Newsletter* 8.3 (July, August, September 2004).

21. Ibid.

Patricia O'Brien

1. UN Department of Public Information. SG/A/1147/BIO/4002 (6 August 2008).

2. UN Office of Legal Affairs website (accessed December 2010).

3. Battel, Roisin. "Ireland's Celtic Tiger Economy." *Science, Technology, and Human Values.* 28.1 (Winter 2003).

4. The Bar Council of Ireland website (accessed December 2010).

5. O'Brien, Patricia. Statement "Peace, Justice and the Rule of Law," delivered at the Georgetown Law Center (Washington, DC, 13 October 2010).

6. Sulaiman, Tosin. "On Top of the World," a conversation with Patricia O'Brien. *Law.com* (1 December 2008).

7. O'Brien, Patricia. Statement "Peace, Justice and the Rule of Law," delivered at the Georgetown Law Center (Washington, DC, 13 October 2010).

8. Ibid.

9. Ibid.

10. Sulaiman, Tosin. "On Top of the World," a conversation with Patricia O'Brien. *Law.com* (1 December 2008).

About the Authors

Avril David is a writer who works in leadership development for a global consulting firm.

Shana Sung is an environmental policy expert who works at the United Nations.

It is the authors' hope that when people read this book, no matter how old they are or where they are from, they will see these stories as a source of inspiration for their own lives. They also hope that through these stories, readers will gain a deeper understanding of the United Nations' work and, along with it, some of the global challenges that we face together.

Thank you for your contribution...

Twenty percent of the proceeds from every book sold will be donated to an international children's charity that supports girls' education.